RE-BEGIN AT ZERO

CLEARING BELIEFS, BIASES AND BAGGAGE TO LIVE ONLY TODAY

SACHIIN GOEL

First Edition 2025

ISBN 978-93-343-8561-8

Published by Sachiin Goel

ACKNOWLEDGEMENTS

Writing "Re-Begin at Zero" has been a deeply personal and transformative journey. I am immensely grateful to those who have supported and inspired me along the way.

First and foremost, I would like to thank the Divine energy that inspired and guided me throughout this process. Your presence has been a constant source of strength and creativity.

To my family, thank you for your unwavering love and encouragement. Your belief in me has been a constant source of motivation.

To my friends, thank you for your patience and understanding during the times when I was engrossed in writing. Your companionship and support have been invaluable.

Lastly, I would like to thank my readers. Your curiosity and willingness to explore new ideas are what make this journey worthwhile. I hope "Re-Begin at Zero" resonates with you and inspires you to embrace the present moment with an open heart.

With gratitude, Sachiin Goel

CONTENTS

INTRODUCTION

In a world where the past clings like a shadow and the future looms with uncertainty, there lies a transformative potential in the present moment—a potential often overshadowed by the weight of beliefs, biases, and the baggage we carry. "Re-Begin at Zero" invites readers to explore the liberating concept of living solely in today, free from the constraints of preconceived notions and inherited narratives that shape our perceptions and actions.

This book delves into the intricate web of convictions that guide our lives, often unconsciously. These beliefs, deeply ingrained and rarely questioned, can dictate our responses and limit our possibilities. By unravelling these threads, we can begin to see the world with fresh eyes, untangling the complexities of our personal and collective experiences.

The subtitle, "Clearing Beliefs, Biases and Baggage to Live Only Today," serves as a guiding beacon for those ready to shed the layers of accumulated thoughts and emotions that hinder authentic living. It speaks to the possibility of a life unencumbered by the burdens of yesterday or the anxieties of tomorrow—a life where each day is an opportunity to start anew, grounded in the simplicity and purity of the present.

Through introspective exercises, thought-provoking insights, and real-life stories, this book offers a roadmap to self-awareness and renewal. It challenges readers to question the validity of their assumptions and to recognize the biases that colour their interactions with the world. As these barriers dissolve, the path to living fully in the present becomes clearer, opening up a realm of possibilities previously obscured by the fog of past experiences and future expectations.

The journey of "Re-Begin at Zero" is one of introspection and liberation, prompting a revaluation of what truly matters. It urges a profound shift in perspective, one that embraces the essence of today, untainted by the residue of past mistakes or future fears. In doing so, it offers a profound invitation to live with intention, presence, and a renewed sense of wonder for the world as it unfolds moment by moment.

Chapter 1: The Prelude of Emptiness

Awakening in the Void

In the silent embrace of nothingness, consciousness flickers into existence. The vast expanse of the void stretches infinitely, an unbroken canvas of potentiality. Here, in this ethereal realm, the absence of form and structure is paradoxically rich with the promise of creation. It is in this boundless space that the soul begins its quiet stirrings, an awakening that reverberates with the echo of beginnings yet to be shaped.

The void, an enigmatic tapestry woven from shadows and whispers, offers a peculiar solace. It is a realm where time loses its linearity, where past, present, and future intertwine in a dance of possibilities. Within this timeless cocoon, the soul finds itself suspended, untouched by the constraints of the tangible world. There is a profound stillness here, a serene pause that invites reflection and introspection.

In this state of suspended animation, the soul becomes acutely aware of its own essence. Stripped of the distractions of material existence, it confronts the raw truth of its being. The void, though seemingly empty, is a mirror reflecting the soul's innermost desires, fears, and aspirations. It is a place where the echoes of one's past choices linger, whispering lessons of growth and transformation.

Yet, the void is not a realm of desolation. It is a crucible of potential, a fertile ground where new beginnings are conceived. Here, the soul is free to explore the myriad paths that lie ahead, unburdened by the weight of expectation. It is a place of liberation, where the shackles of the known are cast aside, and the spirit is free to soar into uncharted territories.

As the soul navigates this enigmatic landscape, it encounters the gentle nudges of intuition, guiding it towards the path of self-discovery. These whispers of insight, like stars scattered across the night sky, illuminate the way forward. In the void, the soul learns to trust its inner wisdom, to listen to the quiet voice that speaks of truth and authenticity.

The awakening in the void is a journey of reclamation, a return to the essence of one's true self. It is a reminder that within the vastness of nothingness lies the seed of everything. Here, in this sacred space, the soul is free to redefine its purpose, to craft a narrative that resonates with its deepest calling.

In the quietude of the void, the soul finds its anchor, a steadfast presence amidst the ebb and flow of existence. It is a place of profound stillness, where the noise of the world fades into the background, and the symphony of one's own heartbeat becomes the guiding rhythm. In this awakening, the soul discovers the power of presence, the gift of being fully immersed in the moment.

Thus, the void becomes a sanctuary, a sacred space where the soul can pause, reflect, and ultimately, re-begin at zero. It is here, in this realm of infinite possibility, that the soul finds the courage to embrace the unknown, to forge a path that is uniquely its own. And as the soul steps forward into the light of a new dawn, it carries with it the wisdom of the void, a reminder that within the stillness lies the potential for endless creation.

The Weight of Nothingness

In the silent crevices of our existence, where the cacophony of life pauses momentarily, we often encounter the profound emptiness that echoes within. This void, this nothingness, is not merely an absence but a presence in itself, a paradoxical weight that both burdens and liberates.

As we stand on the precipice of this void, we may find ourselves grappling with the intangible heaviness it imposes. It is a weight that presses upon the soul, whispering the fears and doubts that we often strive to silence. Yet, within its embrace, there lies a peculiar comfort, a sanctuary where the chaos of the external world fades into obscurity.

Nothingness is a canvas, vast and unmarked, where the potential for creation and destruction coexist. It is here, in this boundless expanse, that we are granted the opportunity to confront the essence of our being. Stripped of distractions, we are left to ponder the intricate tapestry of our thoughts, desires, and dreams.

In these moments of introspection, we may discover the latent power concealed within the void. It is a force that compels us to question, to seek, and to redefine our purpose. The weight of nothingness becomes a catalyst for transformation, urging us to shed the layers that confine us and to explore the limitless possibilities that lie beyond.

Yet, the journey through this emptiness is not without its challenges. It demands courage to face the shadows that linger in the corners of our consciousness. It requires resilience to withstand the pull of despair that often accompanies such profound solitude. But it is through this struggle that we gain clarity, a deeper understanding of our true selves.

The weight of nothingness is not a burden to be shunned, but a gift to be embraced. It is an invitation to pause, to reflect, and to rediscover the beauty in simplicity. In this space, we are reminded that it is not the cacophony of life that defines us, but the silent moments in between.

As we navigate through this void, we learn to find solace in the unadorned truths that surface. We become attuned to the subtle symphony of our inner world, where each note resonates with authenticity and purpose. It is here that we are reminded of the interconnectedness of all things, the delicate balance between existence and non-existence.

Ultimately, the weight of nothingness teaches us to appreciate the profound significance of emptiness. It is a reminder that within the silence lies the potential for profound growth and transformation. It is a testament to the resilience of the human spirit, a reflection of our capacity to find meaning in the void.

In embracing the weight of nothingness, we are not diminished, but rather, we are expanded. We become more attuned to the whispers of our soul, more aware of the intricate dance of life that unfolds within us. And in this awareness, we find the courage to re-begin at zero, to embark on a journey of self-discovery and renewal, ever mindful of the weight that anchors us to the essence of our being.

Silence as a Companion

In the heart of the world's cacophony, silence emerges not as an absence but as a profound presence. It is the soft whisper that accompanies our most intimate thoughts, the unspoken dialogue between the soul and the mind. Silence holds space for contemplation, serving as a canvas upon which the colours of reflection are painted.

In moments of silence, we encounter the self, stripped of the external noise that often dictates our pace and direction. It is here, in this sacred stillness, that we confront our truths and acknowledge our vulnerabilities. Silence becomes a mirror, reflecting the depths of our being, revealing layers that are often overshadowed by the din of daily life.

The companionship of silence fosters a unique intimacy with the self. It invites us to listen, not just to the world around us but to the symphony within. In this listening, we find clarity, a gentle unravelling of thoughts tangled by the rush of existence. Silence does not demand answers; it offers comfort in the questions, allowing us to dwell in uncertainty with grace.

Yet, silence can be daunting. It challenges our comfort zones, urging us to confront the shadows we often avoid. In its embrace, we are left with ourselves, unguarded and vulnerable. But therein lies its power. Silence teaches us resilience, granting us the strength to sit with discomfort and find peace in stillness.

As we journey through the landscapes of our lives, silence becomes a steadfast companion. It travels with us, a silent observer to our triumphs and tribulations. In times of joy, it amplifies our gratitude, allowing us to savor the fleeting moments of happiness. In sorrow, it offers solace, a gentle reminder that even in darkness, there is space for healing.

Silence has the power to transform. It is the alchemist of the soul, turning chaos into calm, confusion into clarity. Through silence, we reconnect with the essence of our being, rekindling the spark of creativity that lies dormant beneath the surface. It is in these quiet moments that inspiration blooms, ideas take root, and dreams are nurtured.

Embracing silence as a companion requires courage. It is an invitation to step away from the noise, to disconnect in order to reconnect. It is a call to be present, to engage with life not as a spectator but as an active participant. In silence, we learn the art of mindfulness, the beauty of being fully immersed in the present moment.

The journey with silence is not one of solitude but of connection. It binds us to the world in profound ways, fostering empathy and understanding. In silence, we hear the unspoken stories of others, the shared humanity that unites us all. We learn to listen with intention, to communicate with compassion.

In the tapestry of life, silence is the thread that weaves through our experiences, binding them together in a harmonious whole. It is the gentle reminder that amidst the noise, there is always a space for stillness, a place where we can return to the essence of who we are. Through silence, we find our way back to ourselves, renewed and ready to begin anew.

In Search of Meaning

The path to understanding is often cluttered with questions that linger in the corners of our minds, waiting for the light of clarity to illuminate them. It is in these shadowed spaces, where certainty and uncertainty dance, that the quest for meaning begins. The human experience is a tapestry woven with threads of joy, sorrow, love, and loss. Each thread, a story, a moment, a fragment of who we are and who we might become. As we stand at the crossroads of our own narratives, it becomes imperative to ask: What gives our lives purpose? What fuels the drive to rise each morning and face the world anew?

Reflecting upon the moments that shape us, it becomes apparent that meaning is not a singular destination but a lifelong pursuit. It is found in the whispers of a gentle breeze, the laughter shared with a friend, and the quiet solitude of a starry night. Meaning is not confined to grand gestures or monumental achievements, but often resides in the simplicity of everyday existence. It is in the way we choose to see the world, in the connections we forge, and in the compassion we extend to others.

In the modern age, where the cacophony of voices and the rapid pace of life can drown out our inner thoughts, finding meaning requires intentionality. It demands that we pause, reflect, and listen to the stillness within. It calls for a willingness to confront the discomfort of not knowing, to embrace the ambiguity that life often presents. In this space of introspection, we discover that meaning is not a preordained path, but a journey of our own making.

The search for meaning is deeply personal, yet universally shared. It transcends cultural, social, and geographical boundaries, uniting us in our shared humanity. It is an exploration of values, beliefs, and desires that shape our actions and decisions. It is the courage to ask the difficult questions and to seek answers that resonate with our true selves. It is a reminder that we are not alone, that others have walked this path before us, and that their stories can offer guidance and solace.

As we navigate the complexities of life, the pursuit of meaning becomes a guiding star, a beacon that illuminates the way forward. It encourages us to live authentically, to align our actions with our values, and to find fulfilment in the present moment. It challenges us to look beyond the superficial and to seek depth in our experiences, to find beauty in the mundane, and to cherish the fleeting moments of connection.

In the end, the search for meaning is a testament to the resilience of the human spirit. It is a journey without a map, yet filled with discovery. It is an invitation to explore the depths of our souls, to uncover the truths that lie within, and to live a life that is rich in purpose and intention. As we continue on this quest, we are reminded that meaning is not something to be found, but something to be created, nurtured, and cherished in the tapestry of our lives.

The First Glimmer of Hope

The morning sky stretched wide above, a canvas of muted blues and soft pinks, whispering promises of a new beginning. As the world around me awoke, I found myself standing at the precipice of change. It was a moment both ordinary and profound, where every breath felt like an invitation to step forward into the unknown.

The air was crisp, carrying with it the scent of fresh possibilities. It was as if the universe, in its infinite wisdom, had conspired to offer me a gentle nudge, a reminder that within the folds of uncertainty lies the potential for transformation. This was not a grand revelation, but rather a subtle shift, a gentle murmur that suggested perhaps things could be different.

Over the past months, life had felt like a series of closed doors, each one a testament to what was no longer possible. Yet here, in this quiet moment, there was a sense of openness, a crack in the facade through which light began to seep. It was the first glimmer of hope, a fragile thing, yet resilient enough to cast shadows aside.

The path ahead was not yet clear, but for the first time in a long time, it did not seem daunting. Instead, it appeared as an opportunity, waiting to be explored with a heart unburdened by past failures. The weight of yesterday's mistakes seemed to lift slightly, replaced by a newfound curiosity about what lay ahead.

It was a curious sensation, this burgeoning optimism. It did not demand grand gestures or sweeping changes, but rather invited a quiet introspection. It called for a gentle reevaluation of what truly mattered, encouraging a focus on the small, often overlooked moments of beauty that peppered everyday life.

As I stood there, I realized that this newfound hope was not about dismissing the struggles that had come before, but rather about acknowledging them as stepping stones leading to this very moment. It was about recognizing the strength that had been forged in the fires of adversity, and allowing it to illuminate the path forward.

There was a calmness in this realization, a quiet assurance that whispered, "You are more than the sum of your past." It was a message that resonated deeply, urging me to trust in the process of becoming, to find solace in the journey of self-discovery.

In this tender space, filled with the promise of renewal, I felt a sense of gratitude for the resilience that had carried me this far. The future was unwritten, a blank page waiting to be filled with stories yet to be lived, and I was ready to embrace it with open arms.

Hope, it seemed, was not a destination but a companion, a guiding light illuminating the way forward. It was a reminder that even in the darkest of times, there exists the potential for change, for growth, and for the emergence of something beautiful.

And so, with a heart full of anticipation and a spirit renewed, I took that tentative step forward, feeling the gentle warmth of hope wrap around me like a comforting embrace. The road ahead was uncertain, but it was mine to explore, and that was enough.

Chapter 2: The Echoes of the Past

Whispers from Yesterday

In the quiet moments that linger between dusk and dawn, memories stir like leaves caught in a gentle breeze. They are fragments of a time that once was, echoing through the corridors of the mind with a soft, persistent murmur. These whispers of yesterday, though faint, possess the power to reshape the contours of our present, urging us to pause and reflect on the paths we have traversed.

Life, in its unpredictable dance, has a way of weaving together a tapestry of experiences that both anchor and propel us forward. Each thread, a story unto itself, intertwines with others to create the intricate patterns that define who we are. Yet, amidst the complexity, there exists a simplicity in the act of remembering—a chance to revisit moments of joy, sorrow, and revelation that have sculpted our very essence.

As we sift through these recollections, it becomes apparent that they do not merely belong to the past. Instead, they are living entities, breathing alongside us, shaping our perceptions and guiding our steps. The laughter of a cherished friend, the warmth of a summer's day, the quiet resolve of overcoming adversity—all these are whispers that beckon us to acknowledge their significance. They remind us that even as time marches on, it carries with it the imprints of what once was.

The beauty of these whispers lies in their ability to teach without demanding, to reveal without overwhelming. In their subtlety, they offer lessons that are often obscured by the noise of the present. They invite us to listen closely, to discern the nuances of their message, and to find meaning in the seemingly mundane. Through them, we learn the art of reflection, of looking inward to discover the truths that resonate most deeply within us.

Yet, there is a delicate balance to be struck between honouring the past and dwelling within it. To linger too long in the shadows of yesterday can hinder our progress, trapping us in a cycle of nostalgia that blinds us to the opportunities of today. Thus, it becomes essential to cultivate a mindful awareness, acknowledging the whispers for what they are—guides, not shackles.

In this dance between past and present, we discover the potential for growth and transformation. By embracing the whispers with an open heart, we allow them to inform our decisions, to illuminate the paths we might otherwise overlook. They serve as gentle reminders that even in the face of uncertainty, we possess the strength to redefine our narratives, to begin anew at zero, unburdened by the weight of what has been.

And so, as we stand on the precipice of what lies ahead, we do so with a quiet confidence, fortified by the knowledge that the whispers of yesterday are forever intertwined with the promise of tomorrow. In this delicate interplay, we find the courage to embrace the unknown, to step forward with intention and grace, and to trust that the journey before us is one of infinite possibility.

Thus, in the whispers from yesterday, we find not only echoes of the past but also the seeds of our future—a reminder that in the continuum of time, each moment holds the potential for rebirth and renewal.

Unraveling Memories

In the quiet corners of the mind, where memories lie like scattered leaves, there exists a landscape both familiar and foreign. Each memory, a fragment of time preserved, whispers stories of the past yet often remains elusive to touch. As I sit in the stillness, I find myself drawn into this delicate tapestry, unravelling threads that hold the essence of who I have been.

The act of remembering is a curious dance, an interplay between the heart and the mind. It is in these moments of reflection that the past reveals itself, not as a linear narrative but as a mosaic of emotions, colours, and sensations. Each memory, a brushstroke on the canvas of consciousness, contributes to the ever-evolving portrait of the self.

In the recesses of my thoughts, I encounter memories that pulse with vivid clarity. The laughter of childhood friends echoes in the corridors of time, their faces illuminated by the golden glow of nostalgia. I recall the bittersweet embrace of first love, a tender chapter marked by innocence and discovery. These recollections, though distant, remain imprinted upon the soul, shaping the contours of identity.

Yet, not all memories are gentle in their presence. Some emerge from the shadows, carrying the weight of unresolved emotions. Faces once familiar blur into the background, and voices fade into silence. These memories, like autumn leaves caught in a gust of wind, swirl chaotically, demanding attention yet resisting comprehension. It is in this space of ambiguity that the heart seeks solace, yearning to reconcile the past with the present.

As I navigate this landscape of recollection, I become acutely aware of the malleability of memory. The mind, a master weaver, stitches together fragments of truth and imagination, crafting narratives that serve the present self. In this realization lies both liberation and challenge—liberation in the knowledge that I am not bound by a fixed past, and challenge in the responsibility to discern the truth within my own stories.

In the unfolding of these memories, I am reminded of the impermanence of all things. Time, relentless in its passage, transforms experiences into echoes, leaving only the essence behind. Yet, within this impermanence lies a profound beauty—the opportunity to redefine, to reimagine, and to re-begin.

The journey through memory is not merely an exercise in nostalgia; it is a pilgrimage of understanding. In revisiting the past, I find threads of continuity, moments that have shaped my values, my beliefs, and my dreams. Each memory, whether cherished or painful, offers insight into the complexities of the human experience.

As I sit with these reflections, I am filled with a quiet gratitude for the tapestry of my life. It is a tapestry woven with threads of joy and sorrow, hope and regret, each contributing to the rich fabric of existence. To unravel these memories is to honour the past, to acknowledge its influence, and to embrace the possibility of new beginnings.

In the stillness, I find peace. The memories, once scattered like leaves, now rest gently, a part of me yet free to transform. And in this peace, I discover the courage to step forward, to re-begin at zero, with the wisdom of the past as my guide.

Lessons Unlearned

In the intricate tapestry of life, there are threads of wisdom that, despite our best efforts, remain elusive. The essence of these lessons often lies in their paradoxical nature: they are learned not through understanding but through the very act of unlearning. This realization emerges not from cerebral acknowledgment but from the quiet spaces between thoughts, where the mind surrenders its need for control and simply observes.

The journey of unlearning begins when one dares to question the foundations upon which their beliefs stand. Often, these foundations are laid in childhood, built from the bricks of inherited truths and societal norms. As children, we absorb the world around us with an unfiltered lens, accepting the paradigms presented to us as absolute. It is only later, when these paradigms fail to serve us, that we start to unravel the tightly wound threads of preconceived notions.

In this unravelling, there is a distinct sense of vulnerability. The safety net of familiar beliefs is no longer there to cushion the fall. Yet, it is in this freefall that the most profound transformations occur. Stripped of preconceived truths, one is left with the raw materials of experience, ready to be reshaped into a new understanding. The process is akin to sculpting, where each chip and chisel reveals a new facet of the underlying form.

What we often realize during this process is that many of the lessons we hold dear are not applicable to the ever-evolving present. They are relics of a past that no longer exists, and clinging to them only serves to anchor us in a reality that has moved on. The challenge lies in recognizing which lessons to retain and which to release. This discernment requires a deep sense of introspection and a willingness to confront the discomfort of change.

The act of unlearning is not a linear path but a cyclical one. It requires revisiting old wounds and accepting that healing is not a destination but a continuous process. Each revisit brings with it a deeper understanding, a new layer of insight that adds richness to the tapestry of our lives. It is through this cyclical process that we learn to navigate the complexities of human existence with grace and humility.

In embracing the lessons unlearned, one finds a profound sense of liberation. Freed from the constraints of outdated beliefs, there is room for growth and exploration. The mind becomes a fertile ground for new ideas and perspectives, each one a seed planted in the soil of openness and curiosity. This newfound freedom allows for a deeper connection to the self and to others, fostering empathy and understanding in a world that often feels fragmented.

Ultimately, the lessons unlearned are not about erasing the past but about integrating it into a broader, more nuanced understanding of the present. It is about acknowledging the fluidity of life and the ever-changing nature of truth. In doing so, we find that the greatest wisdom lies not in holding onto what we know but in embracing the unknown with an open heart and an open mind.

Reflections in the Mirror

The mirror, a silent confidant, offers a candid reflection of our outer selves, yet its surface holds the potential to reveal much more than mere appearances. As I stand before it, the mirrored world invites introspection, challenging me to look beyond the physical and delve into the depths of my own consciousness.

This reflective surface, often taken for granted, becomes a portal to understanding one's inner landscape. It is here that I confront the myriad of masks I wear, each representing different facets of my identity. The person staring back at me is both familiar and foreign—a mosaic of experiences, emotions, and choices that have sculpted my current self.

Through these reflections, I consider the moments that have left indelible marks, shaping my perception of self and world. I recall the laughter that once sparkled in my eyes, the tears that etched pathways down my cheeks, and the dreams that danced with abandon in the recesses of my mind. Each memory is a brushstroke on the canvas of my life, vibrant and alive, yet tinged with the sepia of time's passage.

The mirror also serves as a witness to the changes I have undergone, both subtle and profound. It captures the shifting contours of my face, the subtle lines that speak of wisdom earned, and the resilience that has fortified my spirit. In its reflection, I see not just who I am, but who I have the potential to become. It whispers of possibilities yet unexplored, urging me to redefine boundaries and challenge the limitations I have unconsciously imposed upon myself.

Yet, this reflective process is not without its challenges. The mirror can be unyielding, exposing vulnerabilities and insecurities that lie beneath the surface. It demands honesty and courage, requiring me to confront the parts of myself I would rather hide. But in this confrontation, there is liberation. By acknowledging and embracing my imperfections, I find the strength to grow, to evolve, to re-begin at zero with newfound clarity and purpose.

In the quiet moments of reflection, I find solace in the realization that the mirror's image is not immutable. Each day, each moment, offers an opportunity to redefine and reshape who I am. The reflection is but a snapshot, a glimpse into the ever-evolving story of my life. It is a reminder that change is the only constant, and with every breath, I am reborn anew.

Thus, the mirror stands as a testament to the power of reflection—both literal and metaphorical. It invites me to pause, to ponder, and to appreciate the beauty of transformation. It is a call to action, a gentle nudge to step beyond the confines of the familiar and venture into the unknown with an open heart and an inquisitive mind.

In this dance of reflection, I find a renewed sense of purpose and direction. The mirror, once a simple object, becomes a profound tool for self-discovery, guiding me toward a deeper understanding of who I am and who I aspire to be. As I walk away, the reflection lingers, a silent companion on the journey of life, ever present, ever guiding, ever reflecting.

The Shadows We Cast

Standing at the brink of a new beginning, one often overlooks the shadows that trail behind. These shadows, composed of past experiences, forgotten dreams, and unspoken words, accompany each step forward. They whisper reminders of who we've been, shaping who we are becoming. These phantoms of our past are neither inherently good nor bad; they simply exist, weaving themselves into the tapestry of our lives.

As we navigate the path to renewal, it becomes crucial to acknowledge these shadows. They are the silent witnesses to our journey, holding the lessons learned and the growth achieved. In understanding them, we gain insight into the motivations that drive us, the fears that hold us back, and the aspirations that propel us forward.

Life teaches us that shadows are unavoidable. They are cast by the light of our ambitions and desires, forming a contrast that defines the contours of our identity. In moments of reflection, these shadows reveal themselves as integral parts of our being, urging us to confront the unresolved and embrace the unknown.

It is in the silent conversations with these shadows that we discover the strength to confront our vulnerabilities. They challenge us to question the narratives we hold dear and reevaluate the stories we've told ourselves. By facing these shadows with courage and compassion, we peel back the layers of self-deception, uncovering the truths that lie beneath.

Yet, the shadows we cast are not solely reminders of past missteps or regrets. They also serve as markers of resilience and endurance. Each shadow is a testament to the courage it takes to move forward despite uncertainty, to strive for better even when the path seems unclear. These shadows are the echoes of our perseverance, the silent applause for having dared greatly.

In the quiet moments, when the world fades into the background, the shadows offer a unique perspective. They invite us to pause and consider the balance between light and dark, the harmony between past and present. Through this lens, we begin to see that shadows are not obstacles but opportunities for growth and transformation.

As we continue to re-begin at zero, these shadows remain our constant companions. They are the gentle reminders of the journey undertaken, the silent guides that illuminate the road ahead. By embracing them, we allow ourselves to be anchored in our history while remaining open to the infinite possibilities of the future.

In this dance between light and shadow, we find our rhythm. It is a rhythm that acknowledges the past without being bound by it, that celebrates the present while eagerly anticipating what lies ahead. It is a rhythm that encourages us to step boldly into the future, carrying with us the wisdom of our shadows as we forge a new path.

Thus, the shadows we cast become more than mere reflections of where we've been. They transform into the contours of our becoming, the silent architects of our destiny, guiding us ever forward on this unending journey of self-discovery and renewal. In their embrace, we find the courage to begin anew, to re-begin at zero, and to continue crafting the story of who we are meant to be.

Chapter 3: The Canvas of Possibility

Blank Spaces Await

The notion of a blank space evokes both excitement and trepidation. It is an expanse of untouched potential, a canvas waiting to be filled, yet it can also be a reminder of the unknown, fraught with uncertainty. As I sit before it, pen poised, I find myself caught in a delicate balance between these two opposing forces.

Reflecting on the past, I realize that life is composed of a series of blank spaces, moments that call out to be defined by our actions and choices. Each day presents an opportunity to start anew, to rewrite narratives, and to redefine what has come before. The past, with all its experiences, forms the undercurrent of our existence, shaping who we are but not dictating who we must become.

In this moment of reflection, I acknowledge the weight of expectations, both my own and those imposed by others. The blank space can be both liberating and overwhelming; it is the embodiment of limitless potential, yet it also demands the courage to confront the fears and doubts that linger in the recesses of the mind. How often do we hesitate, paralyzed by the fear of making the wrong choice, of tarnishing the purity of the blank space with imperfections?

And then there is the paradox of time. The blank space is both infinite and fleeting, a reminder that each moment is precious and not to be squandered. It serves as a call to action, urging us to seize the day, to fill the space with meaning and purpose. But what meaning do we seek? What purpose drives us? These questions echo in the silence, seeking resolution.

In this reflective pause, I come to understand that the blank space is not just an external entity but an internal one as well. It exists within us, in the spaces between thoughts, in the quiet moments of introspection. It is a place where we can confront our true selves, unguarded and honest. It is where we can explore the depths of our desires, where dreams take shape, and where we can dare to imagine a future unbound by the constraints of the past.

As I contemplate this inner landscape, I recognize that the blank space is not something to be feared but embraced. It is an invitation to reinvent, to create, and to grow. It is a reminder that every ending is also a beginning, that with each step forward, we can redefine who we are and what we aspire to become.

The blank space is a testament to resilience and hope, a symbol of the human spirit's capacity for renewal. It is a canvas on which we can paint our aspirations, a stage on which we can play out our dreams. It is a space where we can confront our limitations and transcend them, where we can find strength in vulnerability and wisdom in uncertainty.

In this moment of contemplation, I resolve to embrace the blank space before me, to fill it with intention and purpose, to let it guide me on a path of discovery and growth. For in the blank spaces that await, I find the promise of endless possibilities, the chance to begin again, to reimagine, and to redefine what it means to truly live.

Colors of the Mind

The tapestry of our thoughts and feelings weaves itself in hues that often go unnoticed in the frenzy of daily life. These colours are not just metaphors but the very essence of our emotional and cognitive landscapes. Within this spectrum, each shade represents a unique facet of our being, reflecting the myriad experiences that shape who we are.

Consider the vibrant reds of passion and determination, surging through us like a river of fire. They ignite our ambitions, urging us to break free from constraints and pursue our dreams with fervour. These reds are the embers that glow in the depths of our souls, waiting for the right moment to burst into flames of creativity and drive.

In contrast, the cool blues of tranquillity and reflection offer a sanctuary from the chaos. They invite us to pause, to breathe, and to delve into the depths of introspection. These blues are the calm waters that mirror our inner worlds, revealing truths that might otherwise remain hidden beneath the surface. They are the whispers of intuition, guiding us with gentle wisdom when the noise of the world becomes overwhelming.

Then there are the greens of growth and renewal, symbolizing the perpetual cycle of learning and transformation. These greens are the tender shoots that push through the soil, reaching for the light. They remind us that every experience, whether joyous or painful, contributes to our evolution. It is in the embrace of these greens that we find the courage to shed our old selves and step into new possibilities.

The yellows of joy and optimism illuminate our paths with their radiant glow. They are the laughter that bubbles up from within, the warmth of connection that binds us to others. These yellows are the sunbeams that pierce through the clouds, reminding us of the beauty and wonder that exist in even the simplest moments. They are the sparks of hope that light our way when darkness threatens to engulf us.

Yet, amidst these vibrant colours, there are the somber greys of doubt and uncertainty. They cast shadows over our minds, challenging our perceptions and forcing us to confront our fears. These greys are the storms that test our resilience, the moments of ambiguity that compel us to question and explore. It is through these greys that we learn to navigate the complexities of life, finding balance and clarity in the midst of confusion.

The interplay of these colours forms a dynamic canvas, ever-changing and evolving. They remind us that our minds are not static, but living entities capable of infinite variation. Each colour, each hue, is a reflection of our journey through the vast landscape of human experience. As we move through life, these colours blend and shift, painting a picture that is uniquely our own.

To recognize and appreciate the colours of the mind is to acknowledge the richness of our inner worlds. It is an invitation to explore the depths of our consciousness and to embrace the full spectrum of what it means to be human. In doing so, we begin to understand the profound interconnectedness of our thoughts, emotions, and actions, and the vital role they play in shaping our reality.

Sketches of Dreams

The quiet allure of dreams often dances in the shadows of our waking world, whispering secrets of aspirations and hidden desires. In the delicate tapestry of life, dreams are the vibrant threads that weave through the mundane, colouring it with shades of possibility and hope. As we navigate the labyrinth of existence, these fleeting visions offer glimpses into the realms of what could be, guiding us toward a more profound understanding of ourselves and our place in the world.

In the stillness of night, when the mind is untethered from the constraints of reality, dreams emerge as ethereal sketches, painted in hues of imagination and longing. They are the silent architects of our inner sanctum, constructing landscapes where the boundaries of the possible are stretched and reshaped. Within these transient moments, we find the courage to explore the uncharted territories of our consciousness, where the seeds of potential are sown.

Dreams are not merely figments of a restless mind; they are the echoes of our deepest yearnings, the silent musings of the soul. They speak to us in the language of symbolism and metaphor, urging us to listen closely and decipher their cryptic messages. In this sacred dialogue, we are invited to reflect upon our desires and fears, to confront the shadows that lurk within and embrace the light that beckons us forward.

The act of dreaming is, in itself, a radical form of creation. It is an invitation to transcend the limitations of the tangible world and to imagine new paradigms of existence. In the realm of dreams, we are free to sculpt realities that defy the constraints of logic and reason, to envision futures that are unbound by the shackles of doubt and despair. Here, we are the artists of our own destinies, wielding the brushstrokes of intention and will.

Yet, as with all creations, dreams are ephemeral, slipping through the fingers of consciousness like grains of sand. Upon waking, we are often left with only the faintest traces of their presence, lingering like the scent of a forgotten memory. It is in these moments of transition, from the world of dreams to the world of waking, that we are called to capture the essence of what we have glimpsed. To hold onto the inspiration they provide, to let them guide us as we forge our paths through the complexities of life.

In the pursuit of our dreams, we must be willing to embrace vulnerability, to confront the fears that threaten to obscure our vision. We must cultivate resilience and faith, trusting that the journey toward self-fulfilment is worth the trials and tribulations that may arise. For in this pursuit, we discover the power of dreams to transform not only our lives but the world around us.

Thus, as we stand at the threshold of possibility, let us heed the call of our dreams. Let us become the architects of our own realities, painting our lives with the vibrant colours of hope and aspiration. In doing so, we honour the sacred act of dreaming, breathing life into the sketches that reside within our hearts.

The Brush of Intention

As the early morning light filters through the half-open blinds, casting gentle patterns across the room, the air is filled with a quiet, contemplative energy. It is in these moments, when the world seems to pause, that the mind is free to wander and weave thoughts into the fabric of intention.

Intention is not merely a fleeting thought or a momentary desire; it is the quiet force that propels us forward, guiding our actions and shaping our reality. It is the brush with which we paint the canvas of our lives, each stroke deliberate and imbued with meaning.

In the stillness, the mind becomes a fertile ground for reflection, a place where the seeds of intention are sown. It is here that we must pause, allowing ourselves to delve into the depths of our desires, to unearth the true nature of what we seek. This introspection is not always comfortable, for it requires honesty and vulnerability. Yet, it is through this process that clarity emerges, illuminating the path before us.

With intention, there is a need for awareness, a conscious acknowledgment of the present moment and the choices it presents. It is an invitation to be fully present, to engage with life in a way that is both mindful and deliberate. As we move through our days, intention acts as a compass, steering us towards our truest selves, even amidst the distractions and noise of everyday life.

There is a profound beauty in living with intention, in crafting a life that is an authentic reflection of our innermost values and aspirations. It is a dance of balance, where the heart and mind come together, creating a harmonious rhythm that resonates with our core. In this symphony of intention, each note is carefully chosen, each beat a testament to our commitment to living purposefully.

Yet, intention is not static; it is a fluid, ever-evolving entity. As we grow and change, so too do our intentions, adapting to the shifting landscapes of our lives. This adaptability is a testament to the resilience of the human spirit, our capacity to transform and reinvent ourselves with each new dawn.

To wield the brush of intention is to acknowledge the power we hold in shaping our destiny. It is a reminder that we are the architects of our own existence, capable of creating beauty and meaning in every moment. As we navigate the complexities of life, let us do so with intention, crafting a narrative that is uniquely our own.

In the gentle embrace of intention, we find a sense of purpose, a guiding light that illuminates our path. It is a reminder that we are not merely passengers on this journey, but active participants, capable of steering our own course. With each stroke of the brush, we paint a vibrant tapestry, a testament to the power of intention and the infinite possibilities it holds.

And so, as the day unfolds and the world awakens, let us carry this intention within us, allowing it to color our lives with the hues of hope, love, and authenticity. For it is in this mindful creation that we truly begin again, at zero, with each new breath.

Crafting a Vision

In the quiet moments of reflection, when the world seems to pause, there arises a unique opportunity to reshape one's narrative. This is where the craft of vision begins, a delicate dance between imagination and intention. It's not merely about seeing a path forward but feeling it resonate within the deepest chambers of the heart.

Vision, in its purest form, is a beacon. It doesn't dictate the exact steps but illuminates the possibilities. It whispers of potential, urging one to listen closely to the whispers of intuition. The process of crafting a vision is akin to painting on a blank canvas, where each stroke is guided by an inner compass, leading to a masterpiece that reflects the essence of one's true self.

The first step in this creative process is to quiet the mind, allowing the noise of the external world to fade into the background. In this sacred silence, the seeds of vision are sown. It is here that dreams and desires, often buried beneath layers of practicality and doubt, begin to surface. They emerge not as grandiose plans but as subtle inklings of what could be.

To craft a vision is to engage in a dialogue with oneself, asking the questions that matter most. What ignites the soul? What is the essence of a life well-lived? These inquiries guide the formation of a vision that is not only aspirational but deeply personal and true.

As the vision takes shape, it is essential to remain open to its evolution. Like a river, it may change course, shift, and adapt to the landscape of life. This fluidity does not signify a lack of direction but rather a responsiveness to the world and oneself. It is an acknowledgment that the journey is as important as the destination.

In crafting a vision, one must also confront the shadows of fear and doubt that inevitably arise. These shadows, though daunting, are integral to the process. They challenge the strength of one's conviction and the depth of one's desire. Yet, in facing them, the vision becomes more resilient, fortified by the clarity that emerges from overcoming adversity.

It is important to remember that a vision is not a solitary pursuit. It is enriched by the connections we foster, the wisdom we gather, and the experiences we embrace. It is a tapestry woven with the threads of shared moments and collective aspirations. In this interconnectedness, the vision gains depth and dimension, transforming from a solitary dream into a shared reality.

Ultimately, crafting a vision is an act of creation, an exercise in hope and faith. It is the courage to see beyond the present, to imagine a future that reflects the highest ideals and aspirations. As the vision unfolds, it becomes a guiding star, illuminating the path towards a life that is not just lived but truly cherished. In this act of creation, there is a profound sense of renewal — a re-beginning at zero, where every moment holds the promise of new beginnings and boundless possibilities.

Chapter 4: The Art of Letting Go

Surrendering the Past

In the quiet solitude of introspection, there lies a subtle yet profound understanding that to move forward, one must first lay down the burdens of what has been. The whispers of the past, though distant, often echo with a clarity that belies their age, influencing thoughts and actions in ways both seen and unseen. To start anew, one must acknowledge these echoes, not as chains that bind, but as lessons that guide.

The past, with its tapestry of experiences, is an intricate weave of joy and sorrow, successes and failures, each thread contributing to the fabric of our present selves. Yet, the weight of regret can anchor the soul, preventing the emergence of new chapters. It is in this realization that the power to release is found. Surrendering the past is not an act of forgetting but one of acceptance, where each memory is gently placed into the context of growth and learning.

There is a quiet strength in letting go, in choosing to see the past not as a collection of missteps but as stepping stones leading to the present moment. Each experience, whether cherished or painful, serves a purpose. It is through this lens that one can redefine past narratives, transforming stories of limitation into tales of resilience and strength.

The process of surrendering the past is akin to the gentle unfolding of a flower, where layers are peeled back to reveal the core essence within.

It requires a deep sense of compassion for oneself, a willingness to forgive the perceived imperfections and misjudgements that have shaped the journey thus far. This act of forgiveness is not just an absolution of the self but also extends to others, acknowledging that everyone is navigating their own path, often carrying their own burdens from the past.

In the stillness of reflection, there emerges a profound clarity—that the past need not dictate the future. It is a liberating thought, one that opens the door to infinite possibilities and uncharted paths. By releasing the hold of the past, the present becomes a canvas for creativity and renewal, allowing the crafting of a future untethered by the weight of bygone days.

This surrender is not a singular event but a continuous practice, a gentle reminder that each day offers the opportunity to begin again. It is a commitment to living fully in the present, embracing the now with open arms and an open heart. As the layers of the past are gently set aside, the essence of who we are is revealed, pure and unburdened, ready to step into the fullness of what is yet to be.

In this space of newfound clarity, the heart finds its rhythm, and the spirit dances to the melody of possibility. It is here, in the surrendering of the past, that the journey to re-begin at zero truly starts, with a renewed sense of purpose and an unwavering hope for the future. The past, once a shadow, becomes a source of light, illuminating the path forward with wisdom and grace. It is in this surrender that the true essence of beginning anew is found, where the past becomes a cherished companion on the journey to becoming whole.

Embracing Impermanence

Life is a series of fleeting moments, each one a whisper in the vast expanse of time. As we navigate our existence, we often find ourselves clinging to these moments, seeking permanence in a world that is inherently transient. Yet, it is in recognizing and accepting this impermanence that we find our true freedom.

In the quiet spaces between breaths, we can sense the subtle shifting of time. It is here, in these pauses, that we come to understand the beauty of the ephemeral. Like the delicate petals of a cherry blossom, life is most vibrant in its transitory nature. It is a dance of beginnings and endings, a symphony of change that invites us to listen closely, to appreciate the fleeting notes that compose our days.

As children, we are naturally attuned to the transient nature of the world. We revel in the brief joys of a summer rain, the fleeting magic of a snowflake melting on our tongues. Yet, as we grow, we often lose touch with this innate understanding. The world urges us to seek stability, to anchor ourselves in what feels permanent, even as it shifts beneath our feet. We build walls of certainty, constructing facades of control in an attempt to shield ourselves from the unpredictable.

But the walls we build can become prisons. In our quest for permanence, we risk missing the vibrant colours of the present moment, the rich tapestry woven by the threads of uncertainty. To live fully, we must learn to let go, to surrender our illusions of control and embrace the flow of life.

Consider the ocean, vast and ever-changing. It does not resist the tides that shape it, nor does it cling to the waves that rise and fall upon its surface. Instead, it flows, it adapts, it moves with grace and power that comes from its acceptance of change. In many ways, we are like the ocean, vast in our potential and shaped by the currents of our experiences. By accepting impermanence, we allow ourselves to flow with life, to find strength in our adaptability.

In the acceptance of impermanence lies a profound liberation. It frees us from the shackles of fear and the weight of expectation. We learn to savour the present, to find joy in the simple act of being. Each moment becomes a gift, a fleeting treasure that we hold lightly, knowing it will soon pass.

This understanding does not come easily. It requires mindfulness, a conscious effort to remain open to the possibilities of each moment. It asks us to release our grip on what was and to welcome what is yet to come. In doing so, we cultivate a deep sense of peace, a quiet confidence in the natural ebb and flow of life.

As we journey through this ever-changing world, let us remember that impermanence is not something to be feared, but rather, a guiding force that shapes the path of our existence. By embracing it, we attune ourselves to the rhythm of life, finding harmony in the dance of change and renewal. Thus, we begin anew, each moment a fresh canvas, inviting us to paint our lives with the colors of possibility.

The Gift of Release

In the tapestry of life, threads of our past often weave tightly into our present. These threads form patterns, sometimes intricate and beautiful, other times tangled and cumbersome. The Gift of Release offers us a unique opportunity to disentangle these threads, allowing for a smoother, more vibrant weave as we continue to create the fabric of our lives.

We carry with us memories, experiences, and emotions that shape who we are. Some of these serve as cherished reminders of joy and triumph, while others may weigh us down with regret or sorrow. The act of releasing these burdens is not about forgetting or discarding them, but about acknowledging their place in our narrative and choosing to move forward without their weight.

This journey of release begins with acceptance. Accepting that the past, with all its imperfections, cannot be changed. It is a part of us, but it does not define us. The power lies in recognizing that we have the choice to let go of what no longer serves our growth. This release is an act of self-compassion, a gentle reminder that we are deserving of peace and freedom.

In the quiet moments of introspection, when the noise of the world fades, we find the space to confront our inner struggles. It is within this silence that we can begin to unravel the knots that have held us captive. Each thread released is a step towards clarity and lightness, a step towards reclaiming our power.

The process is not always easy. It requires courage to face the shadows we have long avoided. Yet, with each moment of bravery, we inch closer to liberation. We learn to forgive ourselves and others, understanding that everyone is on their own path of healing. In this forgiveness, we find the strength to release bitterness and resentment, making room for joy and love to flourish.

As we let go, we open ourselves to new possibilities. The space once occupied by past burdens now becomes fertile ground for new dreams and aspirations. We discover a renewed sense of agency, a feeling that we are not bound by the past but free to create our future.

The Gift of Release is not a one-time event but a continuous practice. It is a conscious choice we make each day to live authentically and fully. We learn to trust the process, to understand that even in moments of uncertainty, we are exactly where we need to be.

In this release, we find a profound sense of peace. The kind of peace that comes from knowing we are enough, just as we are. It is a peace that allows us to engage with the world from a place of love rather than fear. With each release, we become more aligned with our true selves, more in tune with the rhythm of life.

The Gift of Release is a transformative experience, one that allows us to shed the past and embrace the present with open arms. It is a testament to our resilience, a celebration of our capacity to rise above and begin anew, at zero, with clarity and purpose. In releasing, we find not only freedom but also the courage to step boldly into the unknown, ready to embrace all that life has to offer.

Freedom in Forgiveness

Forgiveness is a paradoxical gift, offering liberation not just to the forgiven but more profoundly to the forgiver. In the intricate tapestry of human relationships, the threads of resentment and anger can become tightly woven, creating a fabric of bondage that restricts emotional growth. Yet, within the act of forgiveness lies an unparalleled freedom, a release from the burdens that weigh heavily on the heart.

In moments of deep reflection, the realization emerges that holding onto past grievances is akin to carrying a heavy burden on a journey meant to be light and fulfilling. The chains of grudges and bitterness often bind the spirit, preventing it from soaring to its fullest potential. Acknowledging past hurts is crucial, but allowing them to dictate the course of one's emotional landscape is a choice—one that can be altered by the simple yet profound act of forgiveness.

The process of forgiveness is not a denial or minimization of the pain experienced. Rather, it is an active decision to let go of the toxic hold that the past has on the present. It is a conscious choice to release the grip of bitterness and to allow healing to begin. This journey is deeply personal and often challenging, requiring courage and vulnerability.

The act of forgiving can feel daunting, especially when the wounds run deep or when the other party remains unaware or unrepentant. However, the power of forgiveness lies not in the external validation but in the internal transformation it ignites. By choosing to forgive, individuals reclaim their power, taking control of their emotional well-being and setting themselves free from the constraints of past hurts.

Forgiveness does not imply forgetting or excusing the wrongs committed. It is a recognition that clinging to resentment only serves to perpetuate one's suffering. It is a testament to the strength and resilience of the human spirit, a declaration of the intention to move forward unencumbered by the past. Through forgiveness, individuals can redefine their narratives, transforming stories of pain into those of growth and renewal.

In the silence of introspection, the heart often whispers truths that the mind may struggle to accept. It is in these moments of quiet contemplation that the seeds of forgiveness are sown. As these seeds take root, they blossom into a profound sense of peace and liberation, allowing the spirit to transcend the confines of past grievances.

The freedom found in forgiveness is transformative, a rebirth of sorts, enabling individuals to re-begin at zero—unshackled by the weight of past transgressions. It is a powerful reminder that while the past may shape us, it does not have to define us. Through forgiveness, a new path is carved, one where compassion, empathy, and understanding flourish.

In this newfound freedom, the soul finds its true essence, unburdened by the shadows of resentment. It is a liberating realization that the power to forgive lies within, a gift that, once embraced, offers endless possibilities for healing and growth. As the chains of anger dissolve, the spirit is free to explore the boundless potential of a life lived in harmony with oneself and others.

Releasing the Anchor

The weight of the past can be both a comforting tether and a stifling shackle. As we navigate through life, each experience we encounter adds another link to the chain that binds us. Yet, there comes a time when holding on becomes more burdensome than liberating. It is in these moments that the act of releasing the anchor becomes not just a choice but a necessity for moving forward.

Often, we find ourselves anchored to the familiar, ensnared by memories that, while cherished, may no longer serve our current selves. The anchor, initially a symbol of stability, becomes an impediment to growth. It is crucial to recognize that the past, with all its triumphs and tribulations, is but a chapter in our evolving narrative. To re-begin at zero, one must gently untangle the moorings and allow the vessel of the self to drift toward unexplored horizons.

Releasing the anchor does not signify the erasure of history; rather, it is an acknowledgment of its role in shaping who we are, while consciously choosing not to let it define who we will become. It is an act of courage to let go of outdated beliefs and practices that no longer align with our present reality. This process invites introspection, urging us to sift through the sediment of our past and discern what is worth preserving and what must be cast into the sea.

In this pursuit of liberation, reflection acts as a guiding light. By pausing to examine the weight we carry, we grant ourselves the opportunity to understand its origins and, more importantly, its relevance. We must ask ourselves: What purpose does this anchor serve? Is it a relic of comfort, a vestige of fear, or a beacon of nostalgia? Only by confronting these questions can we begin to loosen the grip of what was, paving the way for what could be.

The process is neither swift nor simple. It requires patience and compassion, both for oneself and for the fragments of the past that cling stubbornly to our psyche. There may be moments of doubt, where the security of the anchor beckons us back to the safety of the known.

However, it is in the willingness to face uncertainty that true freedom lies. By releasing the anchor, we open ourselves to the vastness of possibility, inviting the winds of change to guide us toward new beginnings.

As we set sail anew, we may find that the act of letting go is not an end but a profound beginning. It is an invitation to recreate, to redefine, and to rediscover the essence of who we are. The waters ahead may be uncharted, but they promise a journey rich with potential and purpose.

In this dance between past and future, we learn that it is not the anchor itself that holds power, but our ability to choose when to release it. By doing so, we honour our past while embracing the infinite potential of the present. And in this delicate balance, we find the courage to re-begin at zero, forging paths that lead us toward the heart of who we are meant to be.

Chapter 5: The Journey Inward

Navigating the Inner World

In the quiet corners of our minds, where thoughts drift like clouds across the horizon, lies a landscape teeming with emotions, memories, and dreams. This inner world, often overshadowed by the demands of the external, holds the key to understanding who we truly are. It is a realm of introspection, where the past meets the present, and where the seeds of our future are sown.

To navigate this complex terrain requires a delicate balance of awareness and acceptance. It is about tuning into the subtle whispers of our consciousness, acknowledging the myriad of thoughts that surface, and discerning the patterns that reveal our deepest desires and fears. Here, in this space, we confront the narratives we have constructed about ourselves and the world around us.

The journey inward is not always easy. It demands courage to face the shadows that linger in the recesses of our minds. These shadows, often cast by past experiences and unexpressed emotions, can distort our perception and hinder our growth. Yet, by shedding light on these darker aspects, we begin to unravel the threads that bind us, allowing for a more authentic understanding of our existence.

Reflection serves as a compass in this exploration. It is through reflection that we gain clarity, as if polishing a mirror to see our own reflection more clearly. By embracing both the light and dark within, we cultivate a sense of wholeness, recognizing that each part of our inner world has something to teach us. The process is akin to tending a garden, where we must nurture the soil of our soul, plant seeds of intention, and patiently await the bloom of self-discovery.

In this inner landscape, emotions play a vital role. They are the signposts guiding us towards areas that need attention and healing. Joy and sorrow, love and anger, contentment and restlessness – each emotion carries with it a message, a lesson waiting to be learned. By listening to these emotional signals without judgment, we can begin to understand their origins and address their causes.

Mindfulness becomes an invaluable tool in this endeavour. It is the practice of being present, of observing our thoughts and feelings without becoming entangled in them. Through mindfulness, we learn to witness the ebb and flow of our mental states, cultivating a sense of detachment that allows us to respond rather than react. This shift from reactivity to responsiveness is transformative, granting us the ability to steer our lives with intention and purpose.

As we delve deeper into the recesses of our inner world, we may discover hidden talents, forgotten passions, or new aspirations. It is a place of potential, where the boundaries of what we believe possible can be expanded. By connecting with our authentic selves, we unlock the ability to create a life that is aligned with our true values and aspirations.

Ultimately, navigating the inner world is a lifelong practice, a continuous unfolding of self-awareness and growth. It is an invitation to live with greater consciousness, to honour the complexities of our being, and to embrace the ever-changing tapestry of our inner lives. In this pursuit, we find not only understanding but also a profound sense of peace and fulfilment.

The Compass of Intuition

In the vast landscape of human experience, there exists an enigmatic force, often overlooked, yet profoundly influential—intuition. It is that subtle whisper in the mind, a gentle nudge that guides decisions and actions even when logic stands in opposition. As we navigate the complexities of life, intuition becomes our compass, pointing toward paths that our conscious selves may not immediately recognize.

Intuition thrives in the spaces between thoughts, in the quiet moments where the mind is free from the noise of daily life. It is an ancient wisdom residing deep within, a gift from our ancestors who relied on it for survival long before the advent of reason and rationality. Yet, in the modern world, we often dismiss it as illogical or unfounded, forgetting that it is as much a part of our humanity as reason itself.

Recognizing the value of intuition requires a certain openness, a willingness to trust in the unseen. It demands that we listen not just with our ears, but with our entire being. This is not to say that we should abandon reason; rather, we should allow intuition to complement it, to serve as a guide when the path ahead is shrouded in uncertainty.

The process of tuning into intuition begins with mindfulness. By cultivating awareness of our thoughts and feelings, we create space for intuition to speak. This awareness allows us to discern the difference between the noise of fear and the clarity of an intuitive insight. Often, intuition manifests as a feeling—a sense of peace or unease that accompanies a decision. Paying attention to these feelings is crucial, for they are the language of intuition.

In moments of doubt, when faced with choices that seem equally viable, intuition can provide the clarity we seek. It may come as a sudden insight, a spontaneous idea that feels right even if it defies logical explanation. Trusting these insights requires courage, for intuition does not always align with societal expectations or norms. It calls us to act authentically, to follow paths that resonate with our true selves.

Practicing intuition involves embracing uncertainty. It requires us to let go of the need for concrete answers and to trust the process of discovery. This can be unsettling, especially in a world that values certainty and control. Yet, within this uncertainty lies the potential for profound personal growth. By allowing intuition to guide us, we open ourselves to new experiences and possibilities that might otherwise remain hidden.

As we become more attuned to our intuition, we find that it often leads us to our passions and purpose. It connects us with our inner desires, revealing what truly matters to us. In this way, intuition is not just a guide but a bridge to a deeper understanding of ourselves and our place in the world.

In the end, intuition is a gift—a reminder that there is more to existence than meets the eye. It invites us to explore the mysteries of life with curiosity and wonder, to trust that there is wisdom beyond what we can see or comprehend. By embracing our intuition, we begin to navigate the world with a sense of grace and confidence, knowing that we are guided by a force that is both ancient and profound.

Facing Inner Demons

In the quiet solitude of our minds, the shadows often linger, echoing whispers of doubt and fear. These shadows, our inner demons, are not to be banished or ignored but understood and embraced as part of our complex human experience. They are the reflections of our past, the scars of battles fought within ourselves, and the silent reminders of our vulnerabilities.

Understanding these inner demons requires a willingness to confront them head-on. It is a journey into the depths of one's psyche, where the terrain is both familiar and alien. Here, the mind becomes a battlefield, a place where courage is not the absence of fear but the determination to move forward despite it. In this space, the heart beats with a mixture of trepidation and resolve, each pulse a drumbeat against the encroaching darkness.

As we delve deeper, the contours of these demons become clearer. They take on forms that are unique to each of us—manifestations of insecurities, regrets, and unfulfilled desires. For some, they are the voices that question self-worth, for others, the spectres of past failures. Yet, within this diversity of form, there is a commonality—they are born from the stories we tell ourselves, narratives woven from the threads of our experiences.

In the act of facing these demons, there is a transformation. The stories we cling to, those that have held us captive, begin to unravel. With each thread pulled, a new narrative emerges, one that speaks of resilience and growth. It is in this unravelling that we find the strength to rewrite our stories, to redefine what it means to be whole.

This process is neither swift nor easy. It demands patience and a gentleness with oneself, a recognition that healing is a journey marked by both progress and setbacks. There will be days when the demons seem insurmountable, their whispers deafening. Yet, there will also be moments of clarity, where the light of understanding pierces through the shadows, illuminating a path forward.

In these moments, we learn that our demons, while formidable, are not invincible. They are part of the human condition, a testament to our capacity for emotion and introspection. By facing them, we do not rid ourselves of them, but we learn to coexist with them, to draw strength from their presence rather than be weakened by it.

This coexistence is an act of self-acceptance, a recognition that to be human is to be imperfect. It is a celebration of the beauty found in our flaws, the wisdom gained from our struggles. In this acceptance, the demons lose their power, their whispers fading into the background as we step into the fullness of our being.

As we continue on this path, we come to understand that facing our inner demons is not a solitary act. It connects us to others, to the shared human experience of grappling with one's own shadows. In this shared struggle, there is empathy, a bond forged in the fires of introspection.

Here, amidst the shadows, we find ourselves. The journey may be fraught with challenges, but it is in facing these challenges that we discover the depth of our courage, the strength of our spirit, and the infinite possibilities of what it means to begin anew.

The Sanctuary Within

In the quiet depths of our existence lies a sanctuary often overlooked—a place where solitude and reflection meet to offer solace from the chaotic noise of the world. This sanctuary is not found in remote locations or hidden behind secluded walls, but rather within the contours of our own being. It is a space of profound calm where the echoes of our innermost thoughts can be heard with clarity, and where the whispers of our true selves emerge.

Navigating the complexities of life often leads us to seek external validation, a pursuit that can leave us feeling adrift and disconnected. Yet, within each of us resides the power to find grounding and peace. This sanctuary within is not a destination but a state of being, a cultivated awareness that allows us to reconnect with our essence. It invites us to pause, to listen, and to nurture our spirit in ways that external pursuits cannot fulfill.

As we peel away the layers of societal expectations and self-imposed limitations, the path to this inner haven becomes clearer. It requires a gentle surrender to the present moment, an acceptance of our imperfections, and a willingness to delve into the depths of our emotions. Here, in the quietude, we confront our fears and aspirations, embracing them as parts of our intricate tapestry.

It is in this sacred space that we come to understand the importance of self-compassion. The harsh critic within is softened by the understanding that we are all works in progress, constantly evolving and learning. This inner sanctuary becomes a refuge where we can extend kindness to ourselves, acknowledging our struggles while celebrating our victories, however small.

The journey inward often reveals the interconnectedness of our experiences. We see how our past has shaped us, how our present choices define us, and how our future is a canvas awaiting the brushstrokes of our intentions. In this space, we are reminded that we are not solitary islands but part of a vast ocean of shared humanity. This realization fosters empathy, both for ourselves and for others, as we recognize the common threads that bind us.

In moments of stillness, the sanctuary within becomes a wellspring of creativity and inspiration. Ideas flow freely, unencumbered by the constraints of external judgment. Here, we are free to explore the realms of possibility, to dream without boundaries, and to imagine new beginnings. It is a place where the seeds of transformation are sown, nurtured by the fertile ground of introspection.

To access this sanctuary, one must cultivate patience and practice presence. It requires a commitment to self-awareness and a dedication to nurturing one's inner life. It is a journey without a map, guided by intuition and the gentle whispers of the heart. As we immerse ourselves in this sacred space, we discover that the answers we seek are not found in the cacophony of the world but in the quietude of our own souls.

In this sanctuary within, we find not only refuge but also the strength to face the world anew, with a heart open to possibilities and a mind attuned to the wisdom that resides in stillness. Here, we begin again, grounded in the peace that only an inner sanctuary can provide, ready to engage with life from a place of authenticity and grace.

Finding Inner Peace

In the quiet moments of solitude, when the world falls away and all that remains is the gentle hum of one's own breath, there lies a profound gateway to inner peace. It is a space that exists not in distant lands or hidden retreats but within the very essence of our being. This sanctuary is available to anyone willing to pause, reflect, and listen to the subtle whispers of their own heart.

The path to this inner tranquillity often begins with an acknowledgment of the present moment—a conscious decision to step away from the clamour of daily life and into a state of mindful awareness. Here, every breath becomes a gentle reminder of the simplicity and beauty of existence. In this state, the mind is free from the shackles of past regrets and future anxieties, allowing the soul to rest in the solace of now.

Yet, finding inner peace is not merely about silence or stillness. It is a dynamic dance of self-acceptance and understanding. It requires the courage to face one's own shadows—the fears, doubts, and insecurities that often linger in the corners of our consciousness. By turning towards these aspects with compassion rather than judgment, we begin to unravel the layers that obscure our true self.

This journey inward is deeply personal and unique to each individual. For some, it may be found in the gentle cadence of a morning meditation, where the mind is allowed to wander and return, like waves kissing the shore. For others, it may arise in the rhythmic flow of a creative endeavor, where the act of creation becomes a meditative practice in itself.

Connection with nature also serves as a powerful catalyst for inner peace. The natural world, in its infinite wisdom, offers countless lessons in balance and harmony. A walk through a sunlit forest, the rustle of leaves underfoot, or the sight of a bird soaring effortlessly in the sky can evoke a deep sense of belonging and peace. It is in these moments that we are reminded of our place within the greater tapestry of life.

As we delve deeper into this inner sanctuary, we may encounter the profound realization that peace is not a destination but a state of being. It is not something to be achieved or attained, but rather something to be experienced and cultivated with intention and practice. It is the gentle acceptance of all that is—both within and without.

In this space of peace, we discover the capacity for greater empathy and love, not only for ourselves but for others as well. Our interactions become infused with a sense of calm and understanding, allowing us to navigate the complexities of life with grace and resilience.

Ultimately, the pursuit of inner peace is a journey of coming home to oneself. It is the quiet yet powerful acknowledgment that within the depths of our own being lies a wellspring of serenity and joy, waiting to be tapped into. As we continue to explore this path, we find that peace is not a fleeting moment to be captured, but an enduring presence that resides within us, guiding us gently through the ebb and flow of life.

Chapter 6: Rekindling the Spark

The Fire of Passion

In the quiet moments of our lives, when the world around us fades into a gentle hum, there lies a spark within each of us, waiting to ignite. This spark, often dimmed by the mundane routines and demands of daily life, is the essence of our innermost desires and aspirations. It is the fire of passion that is not easily extinguished, even in the face of life's challenges.

The fire of passion is a force of nature, an intrinsic part of our being that propels us forward, urging us to pursue what truly matters. It is the driving force behind every great achievement and every act of creativity. It whispers to us in the stillness of the night, reminding us of dreams long forgotten and ambitions yet to be realized.

In our pursuit of passion, we often find ourselves at a crossroads, where the familiar path diverges into unexplored territories. It is here, in the realm of uncertainty, that the fire burns brightest, illuminating the way forward with its unwavering light. It is a beacon of hope, guiding us through the fog of doubt and fear.

But passion is not without its challenges. It demands courage and resilience, asking us to step beyond the boundaries of our comfort zones and embrace the unknown. It requires us to confront our fears and insecurities, to stand firm in the face of adversity, and to remain steadfast in our convictions.

As we navigate the complexities of life, the fire of passion serves as a reminder of what is truly important. It calls us to live authentically, to pursue our goals with vigour, and to savour the journey with all its twists and turns. It is a reminder that life is not merely a series of obligations but an opportunity to create, to explore, and to grow.

The fire of passion is a testament to the human spirit, a reflection of our deepest yearnings and our capacity for greatness. It is a call to action, urging us to seize the moment and to live with intention and purpose. It is an invitation to reimagine our lives, to redefine our priorities, and to rediscover the joy of living.

In the stillness of reflection, we come to understand that passion is not a destination but a way of being. It is found in the small moments of joy and in the grand gestures of love. It is present in the quiet determination of a new beginning and in the relentless pursuit of a lifelong dream.

As we stand on the precipice of possibility, the fire of passion beckons us to take the leap, to trust in our abilities, and to believe in the power of our dreams. It is a call to re-begin at zero, to embrace the potential of what is yet to come, and to kindle the flame that resides within us all.

In this space of infinite potential, we are reminded that passion is not merely an emotion but a way of life, a choice to live with purpose and to ignite the world with the brilliance of our dreams. It is the fire that fuels our journey, a testament to the boundless possibilities that await when we dare to follow our hearts.

Nurturing Creativity

In the vast expanse of human potential, creativity often stands as the beacon that guides us toward innovation and self-discovery. Yet, it is a delicate flame that requires nurturing, lest it flickers out under the weight of conformity and routine. Creativity is not merely an innate gift bestowed upon a fortunate few; it is a skill, a muscle that grows stronger with practice and intention.

The first step in nurturing creativity is to create an environment that encourages exploration and curiosity. This involves both physical spaces and mental landscapes. A cluttered mind, much like a cluttered room, can stifle creativity. Simplifying surroundings and mental processes allows ideas to flow freely, unencumbered by distractions. It is in these moments of clarity that the seeds of creativity are sown.

Moreover, creativity thrives on the cross-pollination of ideas. Engaging with diverse perspectives and disciplines can ignite the spark of creativity. By stepping outside one's comfort zone and embracing the unfamiliar, new connections form between seemingly disparate concepts. These connections are the building blocks of innovation, allowing for the birth of ideas that transcend conventional boundaries.

It is crucial to recognize that creativity often arises from the synthesis of knowledge and experience. Thus, nurturing creativity involves a commitment to lifelong learning. This does not solely mean formal education but also a willingness to learn from everyday experiences. Observing the world with a child's wonder, asking questions, and seeking answers in unexpected places enriches the creative process.

Yet, the path to creativity is not without its hurdles. Fear of failure and self-doubt are formidable adversaries that can stifle the creative spirit. Overcoming these barriers requires courage and resilience. Accepting that failure is an integral part of the creative process transforms it from a source of fear into a valuable teacher. Each misstep becomes an opportunity for growth, each setback a lesson in perseverance.

Furthermore, creativity flourishes in an atmosphere of support and encouragement. Surrounding oneself with individuals who value and nurture creativity can be immensely empowering. These are the people who challenge ideas constructively, offer fresh perspectives, and celebrate creative achievements. They are the kindred spirits who understand that creativity is not a solitary endeavour but a collaborative journey.

To nurture creativity, one must also embrace the concept of play. Playfulness invites experimentation and risk-taking, essential components of the creative process. In play, there are no wrong answers, only possibilities to be explored. This mindset encourages a free flow of ideas, unburdened by the constraints of judgment or expectation.

Finally, it is imperative to remember that creativity is a deeply personal and subjective experience. What resonates creatively with one individual may not with another. Thus, nurturing creativity involves honouring one's unique voice and vision. It is about trusting the process, even when the path is unclear, and finding joy in the act of creation itself.

In the end, nurturing creativity is an ongoing commitment to growth, curiosity, and self-discovery. It is a journey not defined by a destination but by the richness of the experiences along the way. As we nurture creativity, we unlock the potential within ourselves to reimagine the world and our place within it.

The Dance of Inspiration

In the quiet moments, when the world seems to pause and the rush of daily life ebbs away, inspiration often finds its way into the heart, like a gentle breeze stirring the leaves of a dormant tree. It is in these moments that the soul begins to dance, awakening to the myriad possibilities that lie ahead. Inspiration is not a force that can be summoned at will, nor is it a fleeting whimsy. It is a profound movement within, a whisper from the depths of our being, urging us to see beyond the ordinary and embrace the extraordinary.

To understand the nature of inspiration is to recognize it as a dance—a fluid, ever-changing choreography that weaves through the tapestry of our lives. It is not a linear path but a spiral, each turn bringing us closer to our true selves. Inspiration is both a guide and a companion, gently nudging us to explore new horizons while grounding us in the present.

There is beauty in the unpredictability of inspiration. It can be sparked by the simplest of things: the laughter of a child, the colours of a sunset, or the rhythm of rain against the window. These moments serve as reminders that inspiration is embedded in the fabric of our everyday experiences, waiting to be discovered and cherished.

To dance with inspiration is to allow ourselves to be vulnerable, to open our hearts to the unknown and trust in the journey it presents. It requires courage to step into the dance, to let go of preconceived notions and expectations, and to move with the rhythm of intuition. In doing so, we become co-creators of our own destiny, shaping our lives with intention and passion.

Inspiration often arrives unannounced, a sudden burst of clarity or a gentle nudge in a new direction. It is in these moments of revelation that we find the strength to break free from the constraints of doubt and fear, to venture into uncharted territories with a sense of wonder and curiosity. The dance of inspiration invites us to explore the depths of our creativity, to push the boundaries of what we believe is possible, and to redefine our own limits.

Yet, inspiration is not a solitary endeavour. It thrives in connection, in the exchange of ideas and the sharing of stories. It is a collective dance, one that transcends individual boundaries and unites us in our shared humanity. Through collaboration and community, inspiration becomes a force for transformation, igniting change and fostering growth.

As we move through life, the dance of inspiration serves as a reminder that we are never truly alone. It encourages us to listen to the quiet whispers of our hearts, to trust in the process of creation, and to celebrate the beauty of our unique journeys. In the dance of inspiration, we find not only the courage to begin again but also the joy of discovering who we are meant to be. And so, with each step, we re-begin at zero, embracing the infinite possibilities that await us.

Fueling the Flame

The essence of beginning anew lies in the ability to nurture the spark that ignites the journey. It is not merely about setting off on a new path but about sustaining the light that guides us through the obscurities of change. This chapter delves into the art of maintaining the vigour and passion that propels one forward, ensuring that the initial enthusiasm does not wane but transforms into a lasting blaze.

Reflecting on the initial moments of inspiration, it becomes evident that they are often fleeting, like a matchstick flaring in the dark. The challenge is in transforming this momentary brilliance into a steady flame. It requires more than mere desire; it demands a conscious effort to feed and protect the fire within. This process is akin to tending to a delicate garden—one must regularly nurture it to witness its full bloom.

In the realm of new beginnings, the mind becomes both ally and adversary. The initial thrill of novelty can quickly give way to doubt and fear. It is vital to cultivate resilience, allowing oneself to confront these emotions without letting them extinguish the flame. This resilience is built through understanding that setbacks are not failures but opportunities to learn and adapt. The fire of determination grows stronger when fuelled by the lessons of past experiences.

Passion serves as the primary fuel, yet it is not inexhaustible. To sustain it, one must continuously seek inspiration from varied sources. Engage in conversations that challenge your perspective, immerse yourself in environments that evoke creativity, and remain open to the wisdom of others who have traversed similar paths. The world is abundant with stories and experiences that can reignite the passion within.

Equally important is the practice of self-care, an often-overlooked aspect of sustaining one's inner flame. The body and mind are inseparable companions on this journey, and neglecting their needs can lead to burnout. Nourish your body with healthy food, engage in physical activity, and allow time for rest and reflection. A well-cared-for vessel will carry the flame further and brighter.

The art of fuelling the flame also involves setting realistic and meaningful goals. Break down larger aspirations into smaller, achievable tasks. Celebrate every milestone, no matter how minor it may seem, for each step forward adds fuel to the fire. This approach not only keeps the flame alive but also builds a sense of accomplishment that motivates further progress.

Moreover, the company one keeps plays a crucial role. Surround yourself with individuals who support and believe in your vision. Their energy and encouragement are vital resources that help keep the flame burning brightly. Conversely, distance yourself from negativity and cynicism that can dampen your spirit.

In the dance of life, the flame of passion and purpose is our guiding light. To keep it alive is to continually seek, explore, and cherish the moments that fuel it. As you embark on new beginnings, remember that the flame within is both fragile and formidable. It is your duty to tend to it, allowing it to illuminate the path ahead, transforming the spark of potential into the fire of reality.

A Blaze of Possibilities

In the quiet moments of solitude, when the world fades into a gentle hum, an extraordinary realization begins to unfurl. It is the understanding that life, at its very core, is a tapestry woven with infinite threads of potential. Each day presents itself as a blank canvas, inviting us to paint our dreams, desires, and aspirations upon it. This is the essence of possibility.

Possibilities are not merely abstract concepts; they are the very substance of our existence. They dwell in the spaces between our thoughts, in the whispers of our hearts, and in the silent promises of dawn. To see them is to awaken to the myriad opportunities that await, shimmering like stars in the vast expanse of our lives.

As we stand at the threshold of each new beginning, we are met with the gentle reminder that the future is not a predetermined path but a boundless field of choices. It is in this moment of awareness that we find the courage to cast aside the shadows of doubt and fear, to step boldly into the unknown. For it is only by venturing into the unfamiliar that we can truly discover the depths of our potential.

The beauty of possibilities lies in their transformative power. They invite us to transcend the limitations of the past and to imagine a future brimming with promise. In this realm, we are no longer confined by the constraints of reality, but are free to explore the contours of our imagination. It is here that dreams take flight, and the extraordinary becomes attainable.

Yet, the journey of possibilities is not without its challenges. It demands of us a willingness to embrace uncertainty and to navigate the complexities of change. It requires us to trust in the process of becoming, to have faith in the unseen, and to believe in the magic of the unfolding. But in this dance with the unknown, we find the essence of growth and the spark of innovation.

In the pursuit of possibilities, we are called to cultivate a mindset of openness and curiosity. It is this openness that allows us to glimpse the infinite potential within ourselves and the world around us. By nurturing a sense of wonder, we become attuned to the subtle nuances of life, and in doing so, we awaken to the richness of our own existence.

As we navigate this landscape of possibilities, we are reminded that each choice we make is a brushstroke on the canvas of our lives. Every decision, no matter how small, contributes to the masterpiece that is uniquely our own. And it is in this act of creation that we find meaning, purpose, and fulfilment.

In the end, the blaze of possibilities is not just a vision of what could be, but a celebration of what is. It is an invitation to live fully, to embrace the present moment, and to revel in the wonder of being alive. For it is within this blaze that we discover the true essence of our humanity, and it is here that we find the courage to re-begin at zero, time and time again.

Chapter 7: The Dance of Relationships

Connections and Disconnections

In the quiet moments between the chaos of daily life, a thought often emerges, unbidden yet persistent. It whispers of beginnings, of the delicate dance between connections formed and those that quietly dissolve into the ether. The interplay of these connections and disconnections shapes not only the narrative of our lives but also the very essence of our being.

Consider the connections we forge—those intricate threads of relationships, ideas, and experiences that weave the fabric of our existence. Each connection serves as a bridge, linking us to moments of joy, understanding, and growth. These relationships breathe life into our days, infusing them with meaning and purpose. The threads may vary in strength and texture, from the gossamer strands of serendipitous encounters to the robust cords of lifelong bonds. In these connections, we find a mirror reflecting our aspirations, fears, and dreams, offering a glimpse into the vast tapestry of human experience.

Yet, as we navigate this intricate web, disconnections are inevitable. They arrive quietly, sometimes unnoticed, until the absence is felt like a missing note in a familiar melody. Disconnections are often born of change, a natural byproduct of growth and evolution. They may stem from a divergence in paths, a shift in priorities, or the simple passage of time. While they may initially evoke a sense of loss or longing, they also hold the potential for renewal and transformation.

In the space left by a disconnection, we find room to pause and reflect. It is an invitation to reassess our values, our goals, and the direction of our journey. This pause, though sometimes uncomfortable, offers clarity and perspective. It urges us to consider what truly matters, to discern the connections that nurture our spirit and those that weigh us down.

As connections fade, the opportunity to re-begin at zero presents itself—a chance to reconstruct our world with intention and awareness. This is not a loss but a recalibration, a chance to align our external relationships with our internal values. In this process, we learn to appreciate the fluidity of life, the ebb and flow of people and experiences that shape our narrative.

The act of reconnection, then, becomes a conscious choice, a deliberate decision to engage with the world anew. It is an acknowledgment of the past, the lessons learned from both connection and disconnection, and a commitment to forging bonds that reflect our authentic selves. In this way, each re-beginning is a testament to resilience, a quiet affirmation of our capacity to adapt and thrive.

Thus, connections and disconnections are not opposing forces but complementary aspects of the human experience. They remind us that life is not a static journey but a dynamic tapestry of beginnings and endings. In embracing both, we find the courage to start anew, to continually re-begin at zero, crafting a life that is rich, meaningful, and profoundly connected.

The Rhythm of Interaction

In the vast symphony of life, human interactions form the melody that guides us through our days. Each encounter, no matter how brief, holds a potential note that can influence our personal narrative. The rhythm of these interactions rarely adheres to a predictable pattern, yet they weave together to create a complex tapestry of experiences.

Reflecting on the nature of these interactions, one realizes that they are not mere exchanges of words or gestures; they are profound connections that resonate with our core. When we engage with others, we embark on an intricate dance of emotions, intentions, and perceptions. This dance requires an acute awareness of the subtle cues that guide us, much like the conductor of an orchestra who senses the ebb and flow of the music.

Consider how a simple smile can transform a mundane encounter into a moment of genuine connection. It is in these small gestures that the rhythm of interaction truly unfolds. A smile is not just a facial expression; it is an invitation to engage, to share in a moment of understanding. It transcends language barriers and cultural differences, becoming a universal symbol of warmth and acceptance.

Yet, the rhythm of interaction is not always harmonious. There are moments when discord arises, when misunderstandings and conflicts threaten to disrupt the flow. These moments challenge us to listen deeply, to attune ourselves to the perspectives of others. It is in these instances that the true art of interaction is revealed: the ability to navigate through discord with grace and empathy.

In our fast-paced world, the rhythm of interaction is often overshadowed by the constant hum of technology. We are connected more than ever, yet genuine connection seems to elude us. The digital age has introduced new dynamics to our interactions, where the immediacy of communication can sometimes dilute the depth of engagement. It is crucial, then, to cultivate an awareness of how we interact in both physical and virtual spaces, ensuring that our connections remain authentic and meaningful.

The rhythm of interaction is also deeply influenced by our internal state. Our mood, mindset, and emotions act as the internal metronome, setting the tempo for how we engage with others. When we are cantered and present, we are more attuned to the needs and feelings of those around us, allowing for a more harmonious exchange. Conversely, when we are distracted or preoccupied, the rhythm can become disjointed, leading to missed opportunities for connection.

Ultimately, the rhythm of interaction is an ever-evolving dance that requires both mindfulness and intention. It invites us to be present, to listen with our hearts, and to engage with empathy and respect. As we navigate this dance, we learn to appreciate the beauty in each interaction, recognizing that every encounter offers a chance to enrich our lives and the lives of others. In this way, the rhythm of interaction becomes not just a melody, but a powerful symphony that shapes our existence.

Building Bridges

In the quiet moments of introspection, the realization dawns that life, in its intricate design, is a series of interconnected pathways. These pathways, though distinct in their purpose, often intersect, forming bridges that guide us from one phase of existence to another. Each bridge, a testament to the resilience and adaptability of the human spirit, offers a passage not just across physical or metaphorical divides, but into realms of understanding previously unexplored.

The construction of these bridges begins with the foundation of awareness. It involves recognizing the gaps in our lives that yearn to be traversed, whether they be emotional chasms, intellectual voids, or spiritual abysses. In acknowledging these divides, we initiate the process of bridging them with intent and purpose.

In the pursuit of connection, the first step is often introspective. It requires a deep dive into the self, an exploration of the fears and limitations that have kept us on one side of the divide. This is a journey of vulnerability, where we confront the shadows that linger at the edges of our consciousness. Yet, in this confrontation, there lies a profound liberation, for it is only by understanding our own depths that we can extend our reach beyond.

Engaging with others is the next critical phase. In reaching out, we extend the bridge of empathy, allowing us to see the world through another's perspective. This act of understanding fosters a sense of unity, dissolving the barriers that once seemed insurmountable. Through dialogue and shared experiences, we lay down the planks of compassion and mutual respect, creating a sturdy platform upon which relationships can flourish.

The process of building bridges is not without its challenges. There are moments when the structure wavers, threatened by the winds of doubt and the weight of past grievances. Yet, it is in these moments that the strength of our foundation is tested and reinforced. Patience and perseverance become the architects of resilience, guiding us to fortify our connections with elements of trust and forgiveness.

As these bridges extend, they become conduits of growth and transformation. They are not mere constructs of passage but are living entities that evolve with each step we take. Every encounter across these bridges enriches our understanding, offering insights that illuminate the path ahead. They are reminders that true progress is not measured by the distance covered but by the depth of connection achieved.

Reflecting on the bridges we build, there is a realization that they lead not just to external destinations but to the core of our being. They are mirrors reflecting our inner journey, revealing the potential for harmony within ourselves and with the world around us. In nurturing these connections, we discover that the essence of life lies not in isolation but in the symphony of interwoven paths.

Thus, the art of building bridges becomes a lifelong endeavor, a continuous dance between solitude and connection. It is a testament to the enduring human spirit, ever striving to transcend boundaries and embrace the infinite possibilities that lie beyond. Through this dance, we re-begin at zero, each step a new beginning, each bridge a promise of discovery.

The Symphony of Understanding

In the quiet moments that punctuate our lives, there is a profound opportunity to engage with the world and ourselves in a richer, more meaningful way. As we traverse the landscapes of our experiences, we find that understanding is not a destination but a dynamic, living entity, akin to a symphony that unfolds with each note revealing layers of depth and nuance.

Understanding begins with listening, not just to the words spoken by others but to the silence that often carries more weight than any utterance. It's in the pauses, the spaces between words, where true comprehension takes root. In these gaps, we can hear the echoes of shared humanity, the unspoken emotions, and the intentions that lie beneath the surface. This active engagement with silence allows us to perceive the world in its full spectrum, where every shade and hue contributes to the grand composition of life.

Moreover, understanding flourishes when we allow ourselves to be vulnerable. To truly grasp the essence of another's experience, we must first confront our own biases and fears, stripping away the armour that shields us from discomfort. This process is neither easy nor swift, but it is necessary. Like a symphony, understanding is composed of movements — some are gentle and soothing, while others are tumultuous and challenging. Each movement demands a willingness to be open, to feel deeply, and to connect authentically.

The beauty of understanding lies in its ability to transform. When we extend our empathy and insight beyond ourselves, we create connections that transcend barriers. These connections are the harmonies that bind us together, weaving a tapestry of shared experiences and collective wisdom. In this interconnectedness, we find that understanding is not a solitary endeavour but a communal journey, where each person contributes a unique voice to the chorus.

As we cultivate a deeper understanding, we begin to see the world through a kaleidoscope of perspectives. Each viewpoint adds a new dimension to our comprehension, inviting us to explore the intricacies of different cultures, beliefs, and experiences. In this exploration, we discover that understanding is not a static state but an ever-evolving process that requires continuous reflection and adaptation.

The symphony of understanding is also a celebration of diversity. It acknowledges that our differences enrich the human experience, offering a broader palette from which to draw meaning and insight. By embracing this diversity, we honour the complexity of existence and recognize that every individual has something valuable to contribute to the grand narrative of life.

In this chapter of understanding, we find that the symphony is not complete without the inclusion of every voice, every story, and every emotion. It is a testament to the power of empathy and the resilience of the human spirit. As we listen, learn, and grow, we become co-creators of this symphony, shaping a world where understanding is not just an ideal but a lived reality. Here, in the symphony of understanding, we find the harmony that unites us all.

Harmony in Diversity

In the vast tapestry of life, each thread contributes to the overall beauty and strength of the fabric. The world, with its myriad cultures, languages, and traditions, is a testament to the richness that diversity brings. Recognizing and appreciating this diversity is akin to discovering a symphony, where each instrument plays its unique part, yet together they create a harmonious melody that resonates deeply within us.

As we navigate the complexities of our interconnected world, it becomes essential to cultivate an environment where differences are celebrated rather than merely tolerated. This requires a shift in perspective—a move from seeing diversity as a challenge to viewing it as an opportunity for growth and enlightenment. It is in this space of acceptance and understanding that true harmony can flourish.

Reflecting on our personal experiences, we often find that the moments that stand out are those where we encountered something or someone different from ourselves. These interactions have the power to broaden our horizons, challenge our preconceived notions, and enrich our understanding of the world. Diversity, in this sense, acts as a mirror, reflecting back to us the limitless possibilities of human expression and creativity.

Building harmony in diversity is not a passive process. It requires active engagement, open-mindedness, and a willingness to listen with empathy. It involves recognizing the value of each individual's contribution and acknowledging that every voice matters. In doing so, we create a space where everyone feels respected and valued, fostering a sense of belonging that transcends superficial differences.

The journey towards harmony in diversity is also deeply personal. It calls for introspection and a commitment to personal growth. As we become more aware of our own biases and assumptions, we can begin to dismantle the barriers that prevent us from fully embracing the richness of diversity around us. This process can be uncomfortable at times, as it challenges us to confront our own limitations and expand our understanding.

In the broader context, harmony in diversity has profound implications for society as a whole. It lays the foundation for innovation, creativity, and progress. When diverse perspectives are brought together, they can lead to groundbreaking ideas and solutions that would not have been possible in a homogenous environment. Moreover, it fosters a sense of community and solidarity, where individuals feel empowered to contribute to the collective well-being.

The essence of harmony in diversity lies in the realization that our differences do not divide us, but rather, they unite us in a shared human experience. It is about finding common ground amidst our varied backgrounds and recognizing that, despite our differences, we are all part of the same global community. In embracing this diversity, we not only enrich our own lives but also contribute to a more inclusive and compassionate world.

As we reflect on the significance of harmony in diversity, we are reminded of the potential for unity and understanding that lies within each of us. It is a call to action to not only appreciate the beauty of our differences but to actively nurture and celebrate them. In doing so, we create a world that is not only more harmonious but also more vibrant and resilient.

Chapter 8: The Power of Presence

Living in the Now

The past often clings to us like a shadow, whispering tales of could-have-beens and might-have-beens, while the future teases us with dreams of what might come to pass. Yet, in the symphony of life, it is the present moment that hums the sweetest melody. This moment, this breath, is all we truly possess.

To live in the now is to open oneself to the richness of existence as it unfolds in real-time. It is an invitation to experience life in its entirety, free from the chains of regret and the weight of anticipation. When we reside fully in the present, we discover a clarity and peace that transcends the cacophony of our restless minds.

Consider the simple act of breathing. It is a rhythm we often overlook, yet it anchors us to the present. Each inhalation is a reminder of life's continuity, and each exhalation, a gentle release. By focusing on this natural cadence, we can cultivate awareness and anchor ourselves in the now.

The world around us is a tapestry of sights, sounds, and sensations, each moment offering a new thread to weave into our experience. When we attune our senses to the present, we begin to notice the subtle beauty in the mundane: the warmth of sunlight filtering through leaves, the distant laughter of children, the comforting aroma of fresh coffee. These are not mere details but the essence of living fully.

Yet, living in the now is not synonymous with ignoring the past or dismissing the future. It is about acknowledging their presence and choosing to focus on the present moment. Our past experiences shape who we are, providing lessons and memories that enrich our lives. Our dreams and aspirations, too, are vital, giving us direction and motivation. But it is in the present that we act, make choices, and create change.

Mindfulness is a tool that aids in this practice. By observing our thoughts without judgment, we create a space between stimulus and response. This pause allows us to recognize patterns, understand our emotions, and respond with intention rather than reflex. In this way, mindfulness becomes a bridge that connects us to the present, fostering a deeper understanding of ourselves and the world.

In the hustle and bustle of modern life, it is easy to become lost in a sea of distractions. Technology, with its constant barrage of notifications, pulls us away from the here and now. To counter this, we must cultivate moments of stillness, times when we step back and simply be. Whether through meditation, a quiet walk in nature, or moments of silent reflection, these practices ground us in the present.

Living in the now is an ongoing practice, a continual return to the present as we navigate the ebb and flow of life. It is an art that requires patience and persistence, yet its rewards are profound. As we learn to embrace the present moment, we discover a deeper connection to ourselves, others, and the world. It is here, in the now, that we find the true essence of being, a place where life unfolds in its purest form, moment by moment, breath by breath.

In the gentle embrace of the present, clarity emerges like the first light of dawn breaking through the unseen horizon. Here, in this sacred space, the clutter of yesterday's worries and tomorrow's uncertainties dissolve, leaving only the pure essence of now.

Imagine a canvas, once crowded with chaotic splashes of colour, slowly being cleansed, stroke by stroke, until a pristine white surface remains. This is the art of mindful living—where each moment is a brush dipped in awareness, painting the world anew with vivid, intentional strokes.

Life often feels like a whirlwind, spinning us through a dizzying array of tasks, responsibilities, and expectations. Yet, within this whirlwind lies a still point, a sanctuary of calm that beckons us to pause, breathe, and simply be. Tuning into this stillness is not an escape from life; rather, it is an embrace of its fullest potential.

Mindfulness invites us to savour the richness of each experience, to notice the subtle nuances of our environment, and to engage fully with our senses. Feel the texture of the earth beneath your feet, listen to the symphony of sounds that surround you, and taste the vibrant flavors of each bite. By anchoring ourselves in the present, we unlock a deeper appreciation for the world and our place within it.

Consider the rhythm of your breath—an ever-present companion that carries you through the ebb and flow of life. Inhale deeply, drawing in the essence of the moment; exhale slowly, releasing tension and worry. Each breath is a reminder of the continuity of life, a gentle nudge to return to the now when the mind begins to wander.

Thoughts may flit like butterflies, restless and elusive, but through mindfulness, we learn to observe without judgment, allowing each thought to come and go as it pleases. This practice cultivates a sense of inner peace, a refuge from the storm of mental chatter.

In the stillness of mindfulness, we find the courage to face our fears and the grace to accept our imperfections. It is here that compassion blooms, not only for others but for ourselves. We learn to treat ourselves with the same kindness and understanding that we would extend to a dear friend.

Mindful moments are not reserved for meditation or solitude; they can be woven seamlessly into the fabric of our daily lives. Whether washing dishes, walking to work, or sipping tea, each act becomes an opportunity for mindfulness, a chance to reconnect with the essence of who we are.

As we cultivate this practice, we begin to notice a shift—a deepening of our connection to the world and to ourselves. The mundane transforms into the extraordinary; the ordinary becomes imbued with meaning. It is a gentle reminder that life is not a race to the finish line, but a series of moments, each worthy of our full attention.

In this mindful awareness, we find a wellspring of gratitude, a profound appreciation for the simple joys and the beauty that often goes unnoticed. And so, we continue, moment by moment, mindful and present, finding peace in the space between breaths.

Awareness as a Tool

In the quiet moments of our day, when the noise of the world fades and we are left alone with our thoughts, there lies a powerful opportunity. This opportunity is not hidden in grand gestures or monumental changes, but rather in the subtle art of awareness. Awareness, in its purest form, is the ability to observe and acknowledge the present moment without judgment. It is the tool that allows us to navigate the complexity of our emotions, thoughts, and experiences, offering a pathway to reimagine our lives from a place of clarity and intention.

Awareness is not a destination, but a continuous journey of exploration. It begins with the simple act of noticing—be it the rhythmic rise and fall of our breath, the subtle tension in our shoulders, or the fleeting nature of our thoughts. In this noticing, we cultivate a deeper understanding of ourselves and the world around us. The practice of awareness invites us to look beyond the surface, to delve into the depths of our inner landscape, where the seeds of transformation lie dormant, waiting to be nurtured.

As we develop our capacity for awareness, we begin to see the patterns that shape our lives. These patterns, often rooted in habitual thinking and behaviour, can limit our potential and cloud our perception. By shining the light of awareness on these patterns, we gain the power to disrupt them, creating space for new possibilities to emerge. This disruption is not about force or resistance, but rather about gentle curiosity and acceptance.

The beauty of awareness lies in its simplicity. It requires no special tools or techniques, only a willingness to be present. In this presence, we find the freedom to choose how we respond to life's challenges. Instead of reacting on autopilot, we can pause, reflect, and make conscious choices that align with our values and aspirations. This shift from reaction to response is where true empowerment resides.

Moreover, awareness fosters a sense of interconnectedness. As we become more attuned to our own experiences, we develop greater empathy and compassion for others. We recognize that beneath our individual stories lies a shared humanity, and this recognition cultivates a sense of belonging and community. In this way, awareness not only transforms our personal lives but also ripples outward, impacting the world around us.

To harness the power of awareness, we must approach it with an open heart and a curious mind. It is a practice that requires patience and perseverance, for the path to self-discovery is rarely linear. There will be moments of clarity and moments of confusion, times of ease and times of struggle. Yet, through it all, awareness remains a steadfast companion, guiding us back to the truth of who we are.

In the grand tapestry of life, awareness is the thread that weaves together the fabric of our existence. It is the tool that empowers us to re-begin at zero, to let go of what no longer serves us, and to step boldly into the unknown with a sense of wonder and possibility. As we cultivate this awareness, we find ourselves not only living but truly thriving, embracing each moment with gratitude and grace.

The Gift of Attention

In the quiet moments between the hum of daily tasks and the barrage of digital notifications, there lies a profound opportunity—one that we often overlook in the rush of modern life. This opportunity is the gift of attention, an elusive yet transformative force that has the power to reshape our interactions, our understanding, and ultimately, our very existence.

Imagine a world where every conversation is a symphony of undivided focus, where every glance, every gesture, is imbued with the richness of genuine presence. In such a world, the mundane becomes meaningful, and the ordinary transforms into the extraordinary. Yet, in our current state, attention is a scarce resource, scattered across multiple demands and distractions.

To truly grasp the essence of this gift, one must first recognize the barriers that hinder its presence. Consider the incessant pull of social media, the constant ding of emails, the relentless pace at which we are expected to operate. These elements, though woven into the fabric of our daily lives, often dilute the quality of our attention, leaving us fragmented and disconnected.

The journey to reclaiming attention begins with a conscious decision to slow down. It requires a deliberate effort to pause, to breathe, and to immerse oneself fully in the present moment. This act of slowing down is not a retreat but rather an advance towards a deeper connection with the self and the world around us.

Engaging with another person through the lens of complete attention can feel like discovering a hidden dimension. It is in these moments that we truly listen, not just to respond, but to understand. The nuances of emotion, the subtleties of expression, become vivid and alive. We begin to appreciate the intricate tapestry of human experience, woven with threads of vulnerability, strength, and authenticity.

Attention, when gifted, becomes a catalyst for growth. It nurtures relationships, fostering trust and empathy. It allows us to see beyond the surface, to recognize the depth and complexity of those we interact with. In doing so, we cultivate a space where others feel seen, heard, and valued—a space where genuine connections flourish.

Moreover, the gift of attention extends beyond interpersonal interactions. It is equally vital in our relationship with ourselves. By turning our focus inward, we embark on a journey of self-discovery. We begin to notice the patterns of our thoughts, the rhythm of our emotions, and the whispers of our intuition. This self-awareness becomes a guiding compass, steering us towards a life of intentionality and fulfilment.

Thus, the gift of attention is not just a fleeting moment of focus but a sustained practice that enriches our lives. It is a commitment to being fully present, to engaging with the world with curiosity and compassion. As we cultivate this gift, we unlock the potential to transform our experiences, creating a ripple effect that touches every aspect of our existence.

In embracing the gift of attention, we step into a realm of infinite possibilities—a realm where the quality of our presence defines the quality of our life. It is here, at the intersection of mindfulness and connection, that we find the true essence of what it means to live fully, to begin anew each moment with clarity and purpose.

Being Here, Now

The present moment is a gift often wrapped in layers of distractions and future anxieties. Yet, it is within this moment that true clarity and profound understanding reside. To be truly present is to engage with the world with an openness that is both liberating and enlightening. It is an act of courage to pause and acknowledge the current moment without the burden of past regrets or future worries.

In a world that constantly demands our attention, it is easy to become entangled in a web of perpetual motion. The mind races ahead, planning and predicting, while the heart yearns for a slower, more mindful pace. To be here, now, is to allow oneself to breathe deeply and to appreciate the subtle nuances of existence that often go unnoticed.

Consider the simple act of observing a sunset. As the sun dips below the horizon, it paints the sky with hues of orange and pink, a testament to the beauty of the natural world. To truly experience this moment, one must let go of the mental chatter and the incessant need to capture it through a lens. Instead, feel the warmth of the sun's rays on your skin, listen to the whisper of the wind, and watch as the day gracefully yields to night. This is the essence of being present.

Being here, now, also involves a profound acceptance of oneself. It requires an acknowledgment of one's thoughts, feelings, and sensations without judgment or resistance. This self-awareness cultivates a deeper understanding of who we are and what we value. It invites an exploration of our inner landscapes, where we can confront fears and insecurities with compassion and patience.

The art of presence is not confined to moments of solitude. It extends to our interactions with others, where it fosters genuine connections and empathy. When we engage with others with full attention, we honour their experiences and stories. This mindful communication nurtures relationships and creates spaces for healing and growth.

It is within the present that we find the capacity to transform our experiences into meaningful narratives. Each moment offers an opportunity to rewrite our stories, to let go of limiting beliefs, and to envision new possibilities. The present is a fertile ground for creativity, where ideas can flourish and dreams can take root.

To cultivate presence, one must practice patience and persistence. It is an ongoing process, a gentle reminder to return to the now whenever the mind drifts. Techniques such as meditation, mindful breathing, and grounding exercises can aid in anchoring us to the present. Yet, more than techniques, it is a mindset, a willingness to be vulnerable and to embrace the fullness of life as it unfolds.

In this present moment, there is an invitation to discover the beauty and richness of living authentically. It is an invitation to witness the world with fresh eyes, to savour the simplicity of being alive, and to find peace in the here and now. The journey to presence is not about reaching a destination but about experiencing the depth of life's unfolding tapestry with awareness and gratitude. Here, in this moment, we find our true selves.

Chapter 9: The Courage to Change

Facing the Unknown

In the stillness of dawn, when the world is yet to stir, lies a profound moment of clarity. It is here, in this fragile intersection of night and day, that the weight of the unknown makes its presence felt. The transition from darkness to light mirrors the journey of stepping into uncharted territories, where the lines between certainty and uncertainty blur, and the familiar comforts of the past fade into the background.

Standing at the brink of the unknown is a moment rife with possibilities, yet shadowed by the spectre of fear. It is the fear of losing control, of encountering the unexpected, and of confronting the unyielding truth that not everything can be anticipated or planned. This fear, though daunting, is not an enemy to be vanquished, but rather a companion to be acknowledged. It serves as a reminder that life, in its essence, is an ever-evolving tapestry woven with threads of unpredictability.

As one peers into the abyss of the unknown, it is easy to feel dwarfed by its vastness. The mind wrestles with questions that have no immediate answers, and the heart grapples with the vulnerability that comes with stepping beyond the safety of the known. Yet, within this vulnerability lies a hidden strength. It is the strength of resilience, of adaptability, and of a spirit unyielding in its quest for growth.

Reflecting upon the nature of the unknown, it becomes evident that it is not a void, but rather a canvas waiting to be painted with the hues of experience and discovery. It beckons with the promise of new beginnings, urging one to relinquish the shackles of preconceived notions and to embrace the fluidity of existence. Each step into the unknown is a brushstroke, each moment a splash of colour, contributing to the masterpiece that is life.

In the face of uncertainty, there is a call to trust in one's own ability to navigate the labyrinth of the unfamiliar. It is a call to listen to the quiet whispers of intuition, to lean into the discomfort of not knowing, and to find solace in the knowledge that every journey into the unknown is a step towards self-discovery. The unknown, in its enigmatic beauty, invites a dance with curiosity, urging one to explore with an open heart and an inquisitive mind.

To stand at the threshold of the unknown is to acknowledge that life is a series of beginnings and endings, each chapter a prelude to the next. It is an acceptance that the only constant is change, and within that change lies the potential for transformation. As the dawn gives way to day, so too does the journey through the unknown give way to new insights, deeper understanding, and a renewed sense of purpose.

Thus, facing the unknown becomes not a task to be feared, but an opportunity to reimagine, to reinvent, and to rediscover the essence of what it means to truly live. It is a call to action, a gentle nudge from the universe, reminding us that the unknown is not a destination, but a path to be traversed with courage, faith, and an unwavering belief in the boundless possibilities that lie ahead.

The Leap of Faith

There comes a moment when standing at the edge feels both exhilarating and terrifying. The horizon, a thin line between the known and the unknown, beckons with a whisper that mingles promise with uncertainty. It is the whisper of change, an invitation to step into the realms of possibility.

Yet, how does one summon the courage to leap when the ground beneath feels so comforting, so familiar? It is in this moment of tension between comfort and growth that true transformation begins. The mind, a master of caution, crafts narratives of what could go wrong. But the heart, a vessel of dreams, beats with the rhythm of what could be.

This chapter is about that pivotal moment when one chooses to trust the unseen path. It is about acknowledging the fear that clings to the edges of our aspirations and choosing to move forward despite it. Here, we find that courage is not the absence of fear but the willingness to act in the face of it.

The stories of those who have taken the leap reveal a tapestry of human resilience and ingenuity. One recalls a woman who left a secure job to pursue her passion for art. Her journey was fraught with moments of doubt and financial strain, yet each brushstroke on the canvas was a step towards her true self. The colours she dared to blend were reflections of her willingness to embrace the spectrum of life's possibilities.

Another tale tells of a man who, after years of living in the shadows of expectation, decided to follow his heart. He traded the corporate ladder for a backpack and a ticket to the unknown. The world became his classroom, teaching him lessons in humility, patience, and the interconnectedness of humanity. Each destination was a chapter in his journey towards self-discovery, each interaction a reminder of the beauty that lies in diversity.

These stories, though unique in their specifics, share a common thread: the courage to leap into the unknown. They remind us that the act of faith is not always grand or dramatic. Sometimes, it is as simple as saying yes to a new opportunity, or as profound as choosing to forgive oneself for past mistakes.

In the quiet moments of reflection, we realize that the leap of faith is not just a physical act but a mental and spiritual one. It requires a surrender to the flow of life, a trust in the process of becoming. It invites us to release the grip on control and to embrace the unfolding of our authentic selves.

As we stand at the precipice of change, we are called to listen to the whispers of our dreams, to honour the call of our hearts. The leap of faith is an invitation to dance with possibility, to step boldly into the unknown with the assurance that no matter the outcome, we are stepping towards growth, towards a fuller expression of who we are meant to be.

Thus, the leap is not a destination but a beginning, a re-beginning at zero, where each step taken is a testament to the courage it takes to live a life that is truly one's own. In this embrace of the unknown, we find not just fear, but also the boundless potential for joy, discovery, and transformation.

Transforming Fear

In the quiet moments when the world seems to stand still, fear often finds its way into the crevices of our thoughts. It is a persistent companion, whispering doubts and weaving webs of uncertainty. Yet, in acknowledging its presence, we unlock the potential to transform it into something profound—a catalyst for change, a stepping stone toward growth.

Fear, at its core, is a natural response to the unknown, a primal instinct designed to protect us from perceived dangers. However, in the modern world, where threats are often less tangible, fear can become an overwhelming barrier, preventing us from reaching for our true potential. Recognizing this is the first step in the transformation process.

To transform fear, we must first understand and accept it. This involves peeling back the layers of our emotions and confronting the root causes of our anxiety. Often, fear is born from past experiences, deeply ingrained beliefs, and societal pressures. By bringing these elements into the light, we begin to see them for what they truly are—constructs of our own making, subject to change and reinterpretation.

Once we have acknowledged our fear, the next step is to reframe it. Instead of viewing fear as a hindrance, we can choose to see it as a guide. Fear can illuminate the areas of our lives where we need to focus our energy and attention. It can point us toward the aspects of ourselves that require healing and growth. By shifting our perspective, fear transforms from an adversary into an ally.

This transformation is not about eradicating fear; rather, it is about harnessing its energy and redirecting it in constructive ways. It involves taking small, deliberate steps toward our fears, gradually building resilience and confidence. Each step forward, no matter how small, is a victory in itself, a testament to our courage and determination.

Mindfulness and self-compassion are invaluable tools in this journey. By cultivating a mindful awareness of our thoughts and emotions, we can observe our fears without judgment, allowing them to exist without letting them control us. Self-compassion teaches us to treat ourselves with kindness and understanding, recognizing that fear is a universal experience, a shared aspect of the human condition.

As we continue to transform fear, we discover the power of vulnerability. Embracing vulnerability means opening ourselves up to the possibility of failure, rejection, and discomfort, yet also to the potential for profound connection and authenticity. It is through vulnerability that we find the courage to step into the unknown, to take risks, and to pursue our deepest aspirations.

In the process of transforming fear, we not only reshape our relationship with it but also redefine our understanding of strength. True strength lies not in the absence of fear but in the willingness to face it with grace and determination. It is in the moments of uncertainty that we find our greatest potential, the opportunity to re-begin at zero, to forge a new path, and to create a life that reflects our truest selves.

Ultimately, the transformation of fear is a journey of self-discovery, a continuous process of growth and evolution. It is an invitation to explore the depths of our being, to uncover the hidden treasures within, and to emerge stronger, wiser, and more resilient than before. And in this transformation, we find not only the courage to face our fears but also the freedom to live boldly and authentically.

The Strength in Vulnerability

In the quiet moments when the world around us falls silent, we often find ourselves confronted by a truth we habitually avoid: the truth of our own vulnerability. It is in these moments, stripped of the layers of armour we wear daily, that we come face to face with the raw, unfiltered essence of who we are. Vulnerability is often perceived as a weakness, a chink in the armour that leaves us exposed to the harshness of the world. Yet, within this exposure lies an untapped reservoir of strength.

Vulnerability, at its core, is the willingness to be open, to lay bare our fears, hopes, and dreams without the certainty of acceptance or understanding. It demands courage because it involves the risk of rejection, the possibility of failure, and the fear of judgment. However, it is precisely through this openness that we connect most deeply with others and with ourselves.

In the intricate dance of human connection, vulnerability acts as the bridge that unites us. It is the moment when we say, "I am here, this is me," and in doing so, invite others to do the same. This mutual exchange, this sharing of our truest selves, is where genuine relationships are forged. It is where empathy flourishes and where the seeds of compassion are sown. When we allow ourselves to be vulnerable, we give others permission to be vulnerable too, creating a space where authenticity thrives.

The path to understanding and accepting our vulnerability is not an easy one. It requires a deep, introspective journey into the shadows of our own psyche. It demands that we acknowledge the parts of ourselves we would rather hide away. But in doing so, we begin to understand that these parts, these vulnerabilities, are not our enemies. Instead, they are teachers, guiding us towards a deeper understanding of who we are and what we are capable of.

In moments of vulnerability, we often discover strengths we never knew we possessed. It is in the face of adversity, when our defences are down, that we find the resilience to push forward. Vulnerability teaches us to trust in our ability to adapt and overcome. It shows us that being open to the world, despite the risks involved, is a testament to our inner strength.

Moreover, embracing vulnerability allows us to experience life in its fullest spectrum. It opens us up to the beauty of uncertainty, to the thrill of not knowing what comes next. By letting go of the need to always be in control, we learn to savour the present moment, to find joy in the unpredictability of life.

In understanding vulnerability as a strength, we redefine what it means to be strong. Strength is not the absence of fear or doubt, but the courage to face them head-on. It is the bravery to stand in the light, unshielded, and say, "This is me, and I am enough." Through vulnerability, we find liberation from the chains of perfection and the freedom to be truly, unapologetically ourselves. In this acceptance, we discover a strength that is as profound as it is transformative.

Embracing New Beginnings

In the intricate tapestry of life, there are moments when the threads of our existence seem to unravel, leaving us at the precipice of the unknown. These moments, filled with both trepidation and anticipation, are the birthplaces of new beginnings. They invite us to step beyond the confines of our comfort zones and to embrace the possibilities that lie ahead.

Change is an inevitable part of the human experience, a constant that can be both daunting and exhilarating. It is in these transformative instances that we are called to redefine ourselves, to let go of the past, and to nurture the seeds of what could be. This chapter delves into the art of starting anew, exploring the emotional landscapes that accompany such transitions and the resilience required to navigate them successfully.

The dawn of a new beginning often brings with it a sense of vulnerability. It is a time when the familiar fades into the background, and the future is a blank canvas awaiting our brushstrokes. This vulnerability, however, is not a weakness but a testament to our courage. It is an acknowledgment that growth often requires us to dismantle the old and embrace the uncertainty of the new.

Reflecting on past experiences, it becomes evident that every ending carries within it the promise of a fresh start. Whether it is the conclusion of a chapter in our personal lives, the end of a professional journey, or the closure of a significant relationship, each ending is an opportunity for rebirth. It is a chance to assess what has been learned, to cherish the memories, and to move forward with renewed purpose.

The process of beginning anew demands introspection and self-awareness. It requires us to confront our fears and insecurities, to question our beliefs, and to redefine our goals. It is an invitation to reconnect with our inner selves, to listen to the whispers of our hearts, and to align our actions with our true desires.

In the face of new beginnings, one must cultivate a mindset of openness and flexibility. The path forward is rarely linear, and unexpected detours may lead to the most profound discoveries. By remaining adaptable and receptive to change, we allow ourselves to explore uncharted territories and to uncover hidden potentials.

As we navigate through this phase of transformation, it is essential to foster a sense of gratitude for the past and optimism for the future. Gratitude allows us to appreciate the experiences that have shaped us, while optimism fuels our journey forward. It is a delicate balance between honouring what was and welcoming what will be.

Ultimately, starting anew is a celebration of life's infinite possibilities. It is a reminder that we are not defined by our past but by our capacity to evolve. With each new beginning, we are presented with a blank slate, an opportunity to write the next chapter of our lives with intention and authenticity.

In these moments of transition, we are reminded of the resilience of the human spirit. We are capable of transforming uncertainty into opportunity and fear into courage. Each new beginning is a testament to our ability to rise, to adapt, and to thrive in the face of the unknown. It is a journey of self-discovery, a path that leads to a deeper understanding of who we are and who we are meant to become.

Chapter 10: The Growth of Resilience

Weathering the Storm

The world has a way of altering its course when we least expect it—twisting paths that seemed straight and clear just moments before. As I sit with my thoughts, memories of turbulent times rise like waves crashing against a rocky shore. The storm, both literal and metaphorical, had arrived without warning, consuming the tranquillity I once took for granted.

In the heart of that tempest, the sky was a swirling tapestry of greys and blacks, each cloud a reminder of the unpredictable nature of life. The rain fell with an insistence that mirrored the chaos within, each drop a testament to the turmoil that had suddenly enveloped my existence. As I navigated through this deluge, I found myself contemplating the fragility of certainty and the strength required to withstand the unknown.

There is a peculiar resilience that emerges when one is stripped of the familiar. I began to realize that adversity, while daunting, can also serve as a crucible for growth. Each challenge faced, each obstacle overcome, became a building block in the architecture of my perseverance. The storm was not merely an external force; it was an internal reckoning, a call to examine the foundations of my beliefs and desires.

As the winds howled and the thunder echoed its ominous refrain, I discovered an unexpected ally within myself—the capacity to adapt. It is a skill often underestimated, yet its value becomes apparent in times of upheaval. Adapting did not mean surrendering to the storm's will; rather, it meant finding new ways to navigate its fury, seeking shelter in the eye of the storm where calmness briefly reigned.

In those moments of stillness, I found clarity. The storm, relentless as it was, had stripped away the superfluous, leaving only what was essential. It was a cleansing of sorts, a forced introspection that illuminated the core of my being. I began to discern the difference between what I had thought was necessary and what truly mattered. The storm had become a mirror, reflecting back the essence of who I was and who I aspired to be.

With each passing day, I learned to dance with the storm, to move in harmony with its rhythms rather than resist its force. The journey was not without its struggles, but it was in these struggles that I found strength I never knew I possessed. The storm had not defeated me; instead, it had shaped me into something new, something resilient.

As the skies began to clear and the first rays of sunlight pierced through the clouds, I emerged from the storm with a renewed sense of purpose. The experience had been transformative, a reminder that beginnings often disguise themselves as endings. The storm, in all its chaos, had given birth to a new chapter, a re-beginning at zero, where possibilities were as vast as the horizon ahead.

In the aftermath, I understood that weathering the storm was not merely about survival. It was about growth, change, and the courage to face the unknown with an open heart. The storm had passed, but its lessons lingered, etching themselves into the fabric of my being, guiding me as I stepped forward into the uncharted future.

Bouncing Back

The moment when everything seems to collapse around you can feel overwhelming, as if the weight of the world is pressing down, suffocating any glimmer of hope. It is in this darkness, however, that the seeds of resilience are sown. These experiences, though painful, forge the strongest of foundations for personal growth.

Reflecting on the times when life seemed insurmountable, it becomes clear that growth often begins at the very point where we feel the most vulnerable. There is an undeniable power in vulnerability—a raw, unfiltered acknowledgment of our current state that opens the door to transformation.

The process of bouncing back is not a linear path. It is a journey marked by setbacks and triumphs, moments of despair followed by unexpected breakthroughs. Each step forward is a testament to the human spirit's capacity to endure and thrive. The key lies in cultivating resilience, an inner strength that allows us to adapt and emerge stronger from adversity.

Resilience is not an innate quality; it is a skill developed through intentional practice and reflection. It begins with the acceptance of our circumstances, acknowledging the pain without judgment or self-pity. This acceptance creates a space for healing, allowing us to process our emotions and understand the lessons embedded within our struggles.

As we navigate through challenges, the importance of perspective becomes evident. Shifting our mindset from one of defeat to one of possibility can transform obstacles into opportunities for growth. This shift is not always easy, requiring conscious effort to focus on what can be learned rather than what has been lost.

Support systems play a crucial role in this process. Surrounding ourselves with individuals who uplift and encourage us provides the necessary foundation for rebuilding. These connections remind us that we are not alone, offering strength and motivation when our own reserves run low.

Amidst the chaos of rebuilding, self-compassion emerges as a vital component. It involves treating ourselves with the same kindness and understanding that we would offer a dear friend. This practice fosters a nurturing environment where healing and growth can occur naturally, free from the harsh criticism that often accompanies failure.

Revisiting our core values and beliefs can also serve as a guiding light, helping us realign with what truly matters. In moments of crisis, these values become anchors, offering clarity and direction when the path forward seems obscured.

Ultimately, the act of bouncing back is a testament to the resilient nature of the human spirit. It is an ongoing process of rebuilding, reevaluating, and renewing our commitment to living authentically. Though challenges will continue to arise, each experience strengthens our resolve, equipping us with the tools necessary to face whatever comes next.

In the end, bouncing back is less about returning to our previous state and more about evolving into a version of ourselves that is wiser, stronger, and more attuned to the beauty of life's complexities. It is in this evolution that we find not only our strength but our purpose, igniting a renewed sense of hope for the future.

The Roots of Strength

In the quiet moments of introspection, when the world falls away and only the stillness of the mind remains, we often find ourselves grappling with the concept of strength. What is it, truly? Where does it originate, and how can we cultivate it, especially when life feels as if it has been uprooted, leaving us exposed and vulnerable?

Understanding the roots of strength requires us to delve beyond the superficial layers of our existence and reach deep into the very core of our being. Strength is not merely the ability to withstand adversity or to power through life's challenges with unwavering resolve. It is, in essence, a profound acceptance of our vulnerabilities and the courage to confront them.

Consider the ancient trees that stand tall in a forest. Their majesty and resilience are not solely defined by their towering presence but by the intricate network of roots that anchor them firmly to the earth. These roots, often invisible to the eye, spread wide and deep, drawing nourishment and stability from the soil. Similarly, our personal strength is nourished by the unseen roots of our experiences, values, and beliefs that ground us.

At times, these roots may be tested by the storms of life—loss, failure, heartbreak. But it is precisely through these trials that we discover the depth of our strength. Just as a tree bends with the wind to prevent breaking, we too must learn to adapt, to be flexible in our approach to life's inevitable challenges. This adaptability is not a sign of weakness but rather an indication of the strength within us to endure and grow.

Cultivating strength begins with self-awareness. It is the conscious recognition of our limitations and the understanding that growth often stems from discomfort. By confronting our fears and embracing the uncertainties that life presents, we nurture the roots of our strength. It is in these moments of discomfort that we learn the most about ourselves, where our true capabilities are revealed.

Moreover, strength is deeply intertwined with our connections to others. Just as roots intertwine beneath the forest floor, providing mutual support and stability, our relationships offer us a network of support. It is through these connections that we find the encouragement and love that fuel our resilience. By reaching out and allowing others to be part of our journey, we reinforce the foundation of our strength.

In the pursuit of strength, it is vital to remember that it is not a destination but a continuous process of growth and discovery. Each challenge, each setback, and each triumph adds a new layer to our understanding of what it means to be strong. It is a journey without end, as dynamic and evolving as the very essence of life itself.

By nurturing the roots of our strength, we not only enhance our capacity to face the storms but also cultivate a life of authenticity and fulfillment. In acknowledging our vulnerabilities, embracing our connections, and remaining open to growth, we uncover an enduring strength that carries us forward, no matter how daunting the path ahead may seem. It is in this understanding that we find true empowerment, grounded not in the absence of fear, but in the courage to persevere despite it.

Adapting to Change

Change, the ever-present companion of life, is often met with resistance and trepidation. Yet, it holds the potential to unlock new paths and opportunities. The human spirit is inherently resilient, capable of navigating the turbulent waters of transformation with grace and wisdom.

Reflecting on moments when the ground beneath us shifts, it becomes evident that adaptation is not merely a response but a skill honed over time. This skill requires a delicate balance between holding onto core values and being open to new perspectives. The art of adaptation lies in the ability to assess the situation with clarity, acknowledging emotions without being overwhelmed by them.

A reflective pause in the midst of change allows for a deeper understanding of one's strengths and limitations. It is within this pause that potential growth is realized. By taking the time to evaluate past responses to change, patterns emerge that reveal what has worked and what hasn't. This introspection enables a more informed approach to future challenges.

In the face of change, flexibility becomes a vital asset. The ability to pivot, to adjust plans and expectations, transforms potential obstacles into stepping stones. This flexibility is not an abandonment of goals but a recalibration of the path to achieve them. It is a recognition that there are multiple routes to success, each offering unique lessons.

Moreover, the role of community in adapting to change cannot be understated. Relationships provide support, perspective, and a shared sense of purpose. Leaning on others for guidance and encouragement fosters a collective resilience that is stronger than individual efforts alone. Engaging with a community also broadens the horizon, offering insights that may not have been apparent in isolation.

The mindset with which one approaches change is crucial. Viewing change as an opportunity rather than a threat shifts the narrative from survival to growth. This mindset fosters curiosity and innovation, encouraging the exploration of new ideas and approaches. It is a mindset that welcomes the unknown with an open heart, ready to learn and evolve.

In moments of uncertainty, grounding oneself in the present can provide stability. Mindfulness practices, such as meditation or journaling, offer a way to center thoughts and emotions, creating space for reflection and insight. These practices serve as anchors, allowing for a calm and measured response to the chaos of change.

Adapting to change is an ongoing process, one that requires patience and perseverance. It is a dance between the known and the unknown, a constant negotiation between comfort and growth. By embracing this dynamic process, individuals can find strength in their capacity to transform and thrive.

In essence, adapting to change is about cultivating resilience, building flexibility, and nurturing connections. It is about recognizing the beauty in impermanence and the potential that lies within each new beginning. Through reflection and action, change becomes not a barrier but a bridge to a richer, more fulfilling existence. It is a testament to the enduring spirit of humanity, capable of rising to meet any challenge with courage and conviction.

The Power of Persistence

In the unfolding tapestry of life, obstacles often emerge as intricate patterns that can seem daunting, yet they are also the very threads that fortify our resolve. As we navigate these challenges, it is persistence that becomes our most steadfast ally, guiding us through the labyrinth of uncertainty and doubt.

The essence of persistence lies in its quiet strength. It is not a loud, boisterous force but rather a steady, unyielding presence that propels us forward, even when the path is obscured by the fog of adversity. It is the gentle reminder that each step, no matter how small, contributes to the journey of transformation.

Imagine standing at the base of a towering mountain, its peak shrouded in mist. The climb may seem insurmountable, yet it is persistence that encourages us to take that first step, and then another, until the summit is within reach. It teaches us to focus on the process rather than the outcome, instilling a sense of patience and resilience that transcends immediate gratification.

In the world of creativity and innovation, persistence is the catalyst for breakthroughs. It is the artist who returns to the canvas day after day, experimenting with colours and forms until a masterpiece emerges. It is the scientist who meticulously tests hypotheses, undeterred by failed experiments, driven by an unwavering belief in discovery. These endeavours are not marked by the absence of failure but by the refusal to be defined by it.

As we reflect on the role of persistence in our own lives, it becomes evident that it is often during our darkest moments that its true power is revealed. When faced with setbacks, it is easy to succumb to despair, to allow doubt to overshadow our aspirations. Yet, persistence whispers in our ear, urging us to rise once more, to trust in our ability to overcome.

This steadfastness is not born from an innate capacity but cultivated through experience. It is the accumulation of every moment we have chosen to persevere, every time we have decided to continue despite the odds. Each of these instances weaves a narrative of resilience, a testament to the strength of the human spirit.

Persistence also fosters a profound sense of self-awareness. As we persist, we come to understand our own limitations and strengths, gaining insight into what truly matters to us. This clarity allows us to prioritize our efforts, focusing on what aligns with our values and aspirations.

Moreover, persistence is a source of inspiration to others. When we witness someone persevering against all odds, it ignites a spark within us, encouraging us to confront our own challenges with renewed vigour. It is a reminder that we are not alone in our struggles, that there is a shared strength in the collective human experience.

As we continue to explore the depths of our potential, let us remember that persistence is not merely an action but a state of mind. It is the quiet confidence that we can endure, adapt, and ultimately triumph. In this way, the power of persistence is not just a tool for personal growth but a beacon of hope, illuminating the path to new beginnings.

Chapter 11: The Influence of Gratitude

The Lens of Appreciation

In the quiet solitude of reflection, a world brimming with unnoticed wonders emerges. It is here, in the stillness of our thoughts, that we begin to perceive the intricate tapestry of life's beauty that often goes overlooked. Appreciation, a gentle yet profound lens, reveals the extraordinary within the ordinary, urging us to pause and absorb the richness of each moment.

Life, in its relentless pace, often sweeps us along, leaving little room for contemplation. The daily routines and responsibilities obscure the subtle marvels that surround us. Yet, by cultivating a mindset of appreciation, we unlock a deeper connection to our experiences and the world at large. This perspective invites us to see the familiar with fresh eyes, turning mundane moments into cherished memories.

Consider the morning sun as it casts its golden glow across a sleepy landscape. Through the lens of appreciation, this daily ritual transforms into a symphony of light and shadow, a dance of warmth and awakening. The aroma of freshly brewed coffee, its comforting steam rising in delicate tendrils, becomes an invitation to savour the present, to acknowledge the simple pleasures that enrich our days.

Appreciation extends beyond the tangible, reaching into the realm of emotions and relationships. It allows us to recognize the silent gestures of kindness, the unspoken bonds that weave us together. In acknowledging the efforts of those around us, we foster a sense of belonging and gratitude, nurturing our connections with authenticity and depth.

This lens, however, requires conscious cultivation. It demands that we slow down, that we resist the urge to rush through life's chapters without pausing to admire the prose. In practicing appreciation, we learn to listen intently, to observe with curiosity, and to engage with sincerity. It is a practice of mindfulness, a deliberate choice to live with awareness and intention.

Through appreciation, we begin to understand that life is not a series of grand events, but rather a collection of small, meaningful moments. Each breath, each heartbeat, carries within it the potential for wonder. The laughter of a child, the rustling of leaves in a gentle breeze, the quiet companionship of a loved one—these are the threads that weave the fabric of our existence.

As we adopt this lens, we also encounter the transformative power of gratitude. Gratitude shifts our focus from what is lacking to what is abundant, from what we desire to what we possess. It is a reminder that fulfilment is not found in the accumulation of material wealth, but in the richness of experiences and relationships.

In this reflective space, we discover that appreciation is not merely an act, but a way of being. It is an invitation to engage with life in its entirety, to acknowledge its complexities and embrace its simplicity. Through appreciation, we re-begin at zero, each moment a new opportunity to witness the beauty that unfolds before us, to cherish the life we are privileged to live.

In this journey of rediscovery, we find that the lens of appreciation not only enriches our own lives but also illuminates the path for others, inviting them to see the world through eyes of wonder and hearts of gratitude. Thus, we embark on a continual cycle of renewal, grounded in the profound simplicity of appreciation.

Counting Blessings

Reflecting on the notion of starting anew often brings to mind the metaphor of a blank canvas. Yet, the reality of life is that we rarely begin from absolute zero. More often than not, we carry with us a complex mosaic of past experiences, emotions, and connections. In this intricate tapestry, blessings are the golden threads that shine most brightly, illuminating our path forward.

Recognizing these blessings requires a shift in perspective—a conscious decision to acknowledge the abundance that surrounds us. It is easy, amidst the noise of daily life, to become entangled in a web of stress and dissatisfaction. However, when we pause and observe, we find that blessings are woven into the very fabric of our existence, waiting to be counted.

Consider the warmth of morning sunlight filtering through a window, casting patterns of light and shadow on the walls. Such moments, often overlooked, are reminders of nature's generosity. They invite us to appreciate the simple pleasures that life offers. Similarly, the laughter shared with friends over a cup of coffee, the comfort of a familiar song, or the quiet strength of a loved one's presence are all blessings that enrich our lives.

In the hurried pace of modern living, it is not uncommon to take these gifts for granted. Yet, by acknowledging them, we cultivate a sense of gratitude that transforms our outlook. Gratitude is more than a fleeting emotion; it is a practice that, when nurtured, fosters resilience and contentment. It allows us to face challenges with equanimity, knowing that we are supported by a network of unseen blessings.

The practice of counting blessings is not merely an exercise in positivity. It is a profound exploration of what truly matters. By focusing on the abundance in our lives, we begin to understand the depth of our connections to others and to the world around us. This realization brings with it a sense of responsibility—to nurture these connections, to give back, and to contribute to the well-being of others.

As we turn inward and reflect on our blessings, we are also reminded of the impermanence of life. Each moment, each interaction, is a fleeting gift. This awareness encourages us to live with intention, to savor each experience, and to hold space for moments of joy and sorrow alike.

In this reflective practice, we find that blessings are not static. They evolve with us, adapting to the contours of our lives. What was once a burden may transform into a blessing with time and perspective. Thus, counting blessings becomes an ongoing dialogue with ourselves, a way to recalibrate and realign our priorities.

In the quiet moments of reflection, we discover that blessings are not always grand gestures or monumental achievements. They are often the subtle, everyday occurrences that, when acknowledged, have the power to shift our perception and enrich our lives. By cultivating an awareness of these blessings, we open ourselves to a more profound experience of life—a life that, even amidst its challenges, is filled with moments of grace and gratitude.

As we navigate the journey of starting anew, let us carry with us the wisdom of counting blessings, for it is in this practice that we find the foundation upon which to build a life of meaning and fulfillment.

The Practice of Thankfulness

In the quiet moments of our lives, when the world seems to pause and the clamour of daily demands fades, there lies an opportunity to cultivate a profound sense of gratitude. This practice, simple yet transformative, invites us to shift our perspective from what is missing to what is present, from lack to abundance.

Thankfulness is not merely an act of acknowledging the good in our lives; it is a deliberate choice to focus on the positive, even amidst adversity. It is the conscious decision to appreciate the simple joys and the fleeting moments that often go unnoticed in the hustle of modern existence. By embracing this mindset, we open ourselves to a deeper understanding of what it means to live fully and meaningfully.

Consider the small wonders that fill each day: the gentle warmth of sunlight streaming through a window, the laughter of a loved one, or the quiet strength of a tree standing resolute against the wind. These are the treasures of existence that, when noticed, enrich our lives immeasurably. To be thankful is to honour these moments, to pause and absorb their beauty and significance.

In practicing thankfulness, one might start by setting aside a few minutes each day to reflect on the gifts life has bestowed. This could be through journaling, where words become a vessel for expressing gratitude, or through silent meditation, where thoughts are allowed to settle and gratitude naturally arises. Each method serves as a reminder of the richness that surrounds us, fostering a sense of contentment and peace.

Moreover, thankfulness extends beyond personal reflection; it is an active engagement with the world. It involves expressing appreciation to others, recognizing their contributions, and acknowledging their presence in our lives. This exchange of gratitude strengthens relationships, building a network of support and kindness that nourishes both giver and receiver.

The practice of thankfulness also encourages resilience. By focusing on what we have rather than what we lack, we build a foundation of positivity that can sustain us through challenging times. It becomes a source of strength, a reminder that even in moments of difficulty, there is something to be grateful for. This perspective can transform obstacles into opportunities for growth and learning.

As we cultivate thankfulness, we may notice subtle shifts in our perception. Colors may appear more vibrant, sounds more melodious, and interactions more meaningful. Life, in all its complexity and beauty, becomes a tapestry of experiences to be cherished. This is the essence of thankfulness—a recognition of the interconnectedness of all things, and an appreciation for the role each plays in our journey.

In essence, thankfulness is a practice of mindfulness and presence. It calls us to slow down, to observe, and to appreciate the world and its wonders. As we embrace this practice, we find ourselves re-centred, with a renewed sense of purpose and joy. In this way, thankfulness becomes a guiding principle, leading us towards a life of fulfilment and peace, where every moment is a gift to be treasured.

Gratitude in Adversity

In the tapestry of our lives, moments of struggle often weave themselves into our narrative, creating intricate patterns that challenge our perception of reality. It is during these times that the essence of gratitude emerges not as a mere sentiment but as a transformative force. When faced with adversity, the mind's natural inclination is to focus on the turmoil, yet hidden within the chaos lies an opportunity for profound growth.

As we navigate through life's turbulent waters, the concept of gratitude can seem elusive, overshadowed by the immediacy of our challenges. However, it is precisely in these moments that gratitude becomes a beacon, illuminating paths we might not have otherwise considered. To cultivate gratitude amid adversity is to shift our perspective, to look beyond the surface of our trials and recognize the underlying lessons they present.

In the eye of the storm, gratitude invites us to pause and reflect, urging us to find value in the seemingly insurmountable. It encourages an exploration of the self, fostering resilience and fortitude. By acknowledging the presence of gratitude, we allow ourselves to transform adversity into a catalyst for personal evolution. It is not about dismissing the gravity of our struggles but rather about recognizing the broader spectrum of our experiences.

The practice of gratitude in challenging times does not demand grand gestures or overwhelming displays of appreciation. Instead, it invites us to find solace in the small victories, the fleeting moments of peace that punctuate our days. Whether it be the unwavering support of a friend, the warmth of a sunrise, or the resilience found in our own hearts, these fragments of gratitude can serve as anchors, grounding us amidst the storm.

In this reflective space, gratitude becomes a dialogue with the self, a gentle reminder of our innate capacity to endure and overcome. It is a testament to the human spirit's ability to find beauty in the midst of chaos, to transform pain into purpose. By embracing gratitude, we cultivate a mindset that embraces the duality of existence, acknowledging both the shadows and the light.

Through this lens, adversity becomes a teacher, imparting wisdom that can only be gleaned through lived experience. It challenges us to redefine our understanding of success, urging us to seek fulfilment not through the absence of hardship but through our response to it. Gratitude becomes the thread that weaves our struggles into a narrative of strength, resilience, and hope.

As we reflect on our journey, we come to understand that gratitude in adversity is not a destination but a continuous practice. It is an invitation to live with intention, to find meaning in the ordinary and the extraordinary alike. In doing so, we transcend the limitations of our circumstances, discovering a deeper connection to ourselves and the world around us.

In embracing gratitude amid adversity, we open ourselves to the possibility that every challenge holds the potential for transformation.

We learn to trust in our ability to rise, to find light in the darkest of times, and to emerge with a renewed sense of purpose and appreciation for the life we are given.

Transformative Thanks

Gratitude is often seen as a simple, even mundane, courtesy that we extend to others. Yet, within its simplicity lies a profound power that can catalyse change and growth. The act of expressing thanks is not merely an acknowledgment of kindness; it is a transformative practice that reshapes our perception and, consequently, our reality.

In the fast-paced world we inhabit, the moments to pause and reflect can feel fleeting. We rush through our days, often overlooking the subtle gifts nestled within each experience. However, when we consciously cultivate gratitude, we begin to notice the threads of connection that weave through our lives. These threads, once illuminated, reveal a tapestry of richness and depth that we might have otherwise missed.

Gratitude opens the door to understanding and acceptance. When we thank someone, we acknowledge their contribution to our lives. This acknowledgment is not just about what they have done, but also about who they are. It is an act of seeing the other person in their entirety, recognizing their struggles, triumphs, and the unique role they play in our shared journey. Such recognition fosters empathy and deepens our relationships, creating a space where transformation can occur.

Moreover, gratitude shifts our focus from what we lack to what we possess. It encourages us to see abundance in the ordinary, to appreciate the small wonders that often go unnoticed. This shift in focus is not just a change in perspective—it is a reorientation of our entire being. By consistently practicing gratitude, we train our minds to seek out the positive, which in turn influences our emotions and actions. This positive feedback loop has the potential to transform not only our outlook but also our reality.

The practice of gratitude also serves as a grounding force. In moments of uncertainty or distress, returning to gratitude can anchor us, providing stability amidst chaos. It reminds us of the constants in our lives—the people, places, and experiences that remain steadfast, offering comfort and support. This grounding effect is crucial in times of transition, helping us to navigate change with grace and resilience.

Furthermore, gratitude has a ripple effect. As we express thanks, we inspire others to do the same, creating a cascade of positivity that extends beyond ourselves. This collective gratitude fosters a sense of community and belonging, reinforcing the idea that we are all interconnected. In this way, gratitude becomes a catalyst for collective transformation, encouraging a culture of appreciation and mutual support.

In essence, gratitude is a tool for transformation. It is both a lens through which we view the world and a bridge that connects us to others. By embracing gratitude, we embark on a journey of continual growth and renewal. We learn to see the extraordinary within the ordinary, to find joy in simplicity, and to cultivate a life rich with meaning and purpose.

The practice of transformative thanks is not just about changing our lives in isolation; it is about creating a ripple of change that touches everyone we encounter. It is a reminder that even in the smallest gestures of thanks, there lies the potential for profound transformation.

Chapter 12: The Symphony of Balance

Harmony in Chaos

In the midst of life's relentless whirlwind, where every moment seems to teeter on the edge of disorder, lies an undeniable beauty—a paradoxical harmony. It is here, amidst the cacophony of existence, that the most profound lessons reveal themselves. This chapter seeks to explore the often-overlooked symphony that resides within chaos, inviting us to reconsider our perceptions and embrace the unexpected.

The human experience is an intricate tapestry woven with threads of unpredictability. Each day presents a new sequence of events, some mundane, others extraordinary. Yet, within this unpredictability lies a rhythm that, if observed closely, offers a sense of balance. It is the interplay of light and shadow, of certainty and doubt, that creates the rich texture of our lives.

Consider the natural world, where chaos often takes centre stage. A storm, with its violent winds and torrential rains, may seem like nature's fury unleashed. However, beneath this turbulent facade lies a mechanism for renewal. The storm clears the air, nourishes the earth, and fosters new growth. Similarly, our personal storms, while unsettling, often pave the way for transformation and growth. They challenge us, forcing us to adapt and evolve.

In a world obsessed with order and control, chaos is often viewed with trepidation. Yet, it is precisely within these moments of upheaval that we find the opportunity to redefine our paths. When the expected dissolves into uncertainty, we are gifted the chance to see beyond the veil of routine, to question our assumptions and redefine our truths. It is in these moments of disruption that creativity flourishes, as we are pushed to think beyond the confines of the familiar.

The art of finding harmony in chaos lies in our ability to be present, to observe without judgment. It requires a willingness to let go of preconceived notions and to trust in the process of life. This acceptance does not imply passivity but rather a conscious choice to engage with the unfolding narrative with an open heart and mind. By doing so, we cultivate resilience, the ability to navigate life's ebbs and flows with grace and strength.

Moreover, chaos teaches us humility. It reminds us of our place within the grand scheme of things, urging us to acknowledge that we are but a small part of a larger, intricate design. This realization fosters a sense of interconnectedness, a recognition that our lives are interwoven with those of others. In understanding this, we find a deeper sense of purpose and belonging.

Thus, the dance between chaos and harmony is not one of opposition, but of complementarity. Each informs the other, creating a dynamic equilibrium that sustains the essence of life. By embracing this duality, we open ourselves to a richer, more nuanced experience, one that honours both the tumultuous and the tranquil.

As we move forward, let us carry with us the understanding that within the chaos lies the seed of harmony. It is a reminder that even in the most disordered of times, there exists a hidden order, a subtle music that, if we listen closely, can guide us towards a more profound understanding of ourselves and the world around us.

Equilibrium of Life

Life, in its essence, is a delicate dance of balance and harmony. This balance is not a static state but an ever-evolving journey that requires constant attention and recalibration. It is about finding the sweet spot where various aspects of our existence coalesce into a harmonious whole.

Often, we find ourselves pulled in myriad directions, each demanding our time and energy. The demands of work, family, personal aspirations, and social obligations can create a cacophony of noise that drowns out the gentle whispers of our inner self. In the midst of this whirlwind, the quest for equilibrium becomes paramount.

To achieve this balance, one must first recognize the interconnectedness of all aspects of life. The physical, mental, emotional, and spiritual dimensions are not separate entities but threads woven into the fabric of our being. Ignoring one can unravel the entire tapestry, leading to a sense of disarray and discontent.

Consider the body as a vessel that carries the mind and spirit. When neglected, it can become a source of imbalance. Nourishing the body with mindful eating, regular exercise, and adequate rest is essential to maintaining its vitality. This physical well-being, in turn, supports mental clarity and emotional stability, allowing for a more centred approach to life's challenges.

Equally important is the cultivation of the mind. In a world bombarded with information, finding moments of stillness and introspection can be a rare luxury. Yet, it is within these moments that clarity emerges. Practices such as meditation, journaling, or simply spending time in nature can quiet the mind and open pathways to deeper understanding.

Emotional equilibrium is another facet of this intricate balance. Emotions are powerful forces that can both uplift and overwhelm. Acknowledging and processing these emotions without judgment is key to maintaining emotional health. This involves understanding the root causes of our feelings and learning to respond, rather than react, to emotional triggers.

The spiritual dimension, often overlooked, is the anchor that grounds us in the present. It is the connection to something greater than ourselves, whether it be through religious beliefs, a sense of purpose, or the awe of nature's beauty. Nurturing this spiritual connection provides a sense of peace and resilience amidst life's uncertainties.

As we navigate the complexities of life, it is crucial to remember that equilibrium is not a destination but a continuous process. It requires patience and self-compassion, acknowledging that there will be times of imbalance. These moments are not failures but opportunities for growth and realignment.

In the pursuit of balance, one must also recognize the importance of setting boundaries. Learning to say no, prioritizing what truly matters, and letting go of what no longer serves us are vital steps in maintaining equilibrium. It is through these conscious choices that we create space for what is meaningful and nourishing.

Ultimately, the equilibrium of life is a personal journey, unique to each individual. It is about finding what resonates with our inner truth and aligning our actions with our values. By embracing this dynamic process, we can cultivate a life of harmony and fulfillment, where the various elements of our existence come together in a beautiful symphony.

Balancing Act

In the midst of life's bustling chaos, there exists a delicate dance between the realms of ambition and contentment. This dance is not a mere routine but a carefully orchestrated performance that requires precision, grace, and an understanding of the rhythm of life. As we navigate this intricate choreography, we often find ourselves teetering on the edge, striving to maintain equilibrium between our personal aspirations and the responsibilities we shoulder.

The notion of balance is not a static achievement but a dynamic process. It evolves with time, shaped by our experiences, priorities, and the ever-changing landscape of our lives. It's akin to walking a tightrope where the slightest misstep can send us spiralling into chaos. Yet, it is in these moments of imbalance that we discover our true selves. We learn to adapt, to recalibrate our steps, and to find our footing once more.

One might question the necessity of such a balancing act. Why not simply choose one path and be done with it? The answer lies in the richness that arises from embracing multiple facets of our existence.

Each aspect, whether it be career, family, or personal growth, contributes to the tapestry of our lives. It is this interplay between different elements that fosters a deeper understanding of ourselves and the world around us.

The pursuit of balance is not without its challenges. It demands a keen awareness of our limits and the courage to set boundaries. This requires introspection and honesty with oneself, acknowledging that it is impossible to excel in every arena simultaneously. There is a humility in admitting that we are not infallible, that sometimes, it is necessary to prioritize and make sacrifices.

Moreover, balance does not imply equal distribution of time and energy across all areas. Instead, it is about being present in each moment, fully engaging with the task at hand, whether it is a work project or a family dinner. It is the quality of our attention that ultimately defines the harmony we seek.

In the quest for balance, one must also be attuned to the signals that indicate when adjustments are needed. Burnout, stress, and dissatisfaction are often signs that we have veered too far in one direction. Recognizing these signs early allows us to make the necessary shifts before reaching a tipping point.

It is crucial to remember that balance is a personal journey, unique to each individual. What works for one may not work for another. It is a process of trial and error, of listening to one's inner voice and finding what resonates. There is no one-size-fits-all solution, and that is the beauty of it.

In this ongoing dance, we find resilience and strength. We learn to sway with the currents of life, to bend without breaking, and to cherish the moments of stillness that punctuate the chaos. This balancing act is not a burden but a gift, an opportunity to explore the depths of our being and to live a life that is rich, fulfilling, and authentically our own. In the end, it is not about achieving perfect balance but about embracing the journey and finding joy in the dance itself.

The Yin and Yang

In the quietude of reflection, a delicate balance emerges, an intertwining dance of dualities that form the essence of our existence. This ancient concept, encapsulated so eloquently by the symbols of Yin and Yang, unveils the inherent duality within every aspect of life. It is a reminder that every beginning is intertwined with an end, every joy with sorrow, and every light with shadow.

As one delves deeper into this philosophy, it becomes apparent that life does not exist in absolutes. Rather, it is a spectrum where opposites are not opposing forces but complementary energies that maintain harmony in the universe. This realization is a crucial step in understanding the cyclical nature of our journeys and the perpetual state of becoming.

Reflecting on the ebb and flow of life, it is essential to recognize the value in both the Yin and the Yang. The Yin, often associated with darkness, passivity, and introspection, invites us to pause and delve into the inner world. It is in these moments of quiet introspection that we find clarity, allowing us to rejuvenate and prepare for the active phases of our lives.

Conversely, the Yang represents the light, activity, and the external expression of our inner truths. It urges us to act, to bring forth the ideas and insights we have nurtured in the shadows into the light of the world. It is this dynamic interplay between introspection and action that propels us forward, enabling growth and transformation.

In embracing this duality, we learn to appreciate the value of each phase. The quietude of Yin is not a void but a fertile ground for seeds of creativity and wisdom to take root. Similarly, the vibrancy of Yang is not chaos but an opportunity to manifest those inner seeds into tangible reality. It is through this continuous cycle that we learn to navigate the complexities of life with grace.

This balance is not static; it requires constant adjustment and awareness. Just as nature adapts to the changing seasons, so too must we adapt to the shifting energies within and around us. By cultivating an awareness of these cycles, we become more attuned to the rhythms of our own lives, learning when to rest and when to act.

The Yin and Yang also teach us about the interconnectedness of all things. In recognizing that one cannot exist without the other, we come to understand that our experiences are part of a larger whole. This awareness fosters a sense of compassion and empathy, as we realize that others are also navigating their own dualities.

Ultimately, the wisdom of Yin and Yang lies in its simplicity and depth. It invites us to embrace the full spectrum of our experiences, to find balance in the midst of chaos, and to seek harmony within ourselves and the world around us. In doing so, we not only find peace within the dualities but also discover the profound beauty that arises from their union. Thus, the journey through the cycles of life becomes a dance of balance, a harmonious interplay of light and shadow, guiding us ever closer to the core of our being.

The Dance of Duality

In the heart of existence, where the pulse of life beats with rhythmic precision, lies a fundamental truth: duality. It is an undeniable aspect of our reality, woven into the very fabric of our being. The dance of duality, with its ebb and flow, compels us to confront the polarities that shape our lives. We find ourselves oscillating between light and shadow, joy and sorrow, strength and vulnerability. This perpetual motion, though seemingly paradoxical, is the essence of growth and transformation.

At times, we may perceive duality as a source of conflict, a battleground where opposing forces vie for dominance. Yet, upon deeper reflection, it reveals itself as a harmonious dance—a dynamic interplay that fosters equilibrium. It is in this tension between opposites that we discover balance and, ultimately, a deeper understanding of ourselves.

Consider the symbiotic relationship between day and night. The sun, in its radiant glory, fills the world with warmth and light, nurturing life. Meanwhile, the moon, with its gentle luminescence, offers solace and reflection. Each serves a purpose, and in their cyclical exchange, they create the rhythm of time. So too in our lives, the interplay of light and shadow invites us to explore the depths of our being, to embrace both our strengths and our vulnerabilities.

In the realm of emotions, duality manifests as joy and sorrow, each an integral part of the human experience. Joy uplifts and invigorates, while sorrow humbles and teaches. Together, they form a spectrum of feeling that enriches our lives. To truly experience joy, we must also understand sorrow; to appreciate the light, we must first traverse the shadows.

The dance of duality extends to our inner landscape, where the mind and heart often tread divergent paths. The mind, with its penchant for logic and reason, seeks order and clarity. The heart, however, is the realm of intuition and emotion, embracing the complexity of human experience. When these two forces align, we unlock the potential for profound insight and wisdom.

In our relationships, duality is ever-present, challenging us to navigate the delicate balance between independence and connection. The desire for autonomy often contrasts with the longing for intimacy, yet both are essential for meaningful interactions. In understanding and respecting this duality, we cultivate relationships that are both fulfilling and liberating.

The dance of duality is not a struggle to be conquered but a rhythm to be embraced. It is an invitation to explore the full spectrum of existence, to delve into the depths of our being and emerge with a more nuanced understanding of the world. By acknowledging and embracing the duality within ourselves, we find the courage to re-begin at zero, to approach life with renewed curiosity and openness.

In this dance, we learn that duality is not a division but a union, a dynamic interplay that propels us forward. It is the pulse of life itself, a reminder that within every end lies a new beginning, and within every challenge, the seed of growth. The dance of duality invites us to revel in the complexity of existence, to find beauty in contrast, and to celebrate the infinite possibilities that arise when we dare to embrace the whole of who we are.

Chapter 13: The Vision of Clarity

Seeing Through the Fog

The morning lay heavy with mist, a dense fog that seemed to wrap around everything like a shroud. As I stepped out, the world felt muffled, as though the fog had absorbed sound and light, leaving behind a surreal stillness. It was a moment that mirrored the state of my mind—clouded, searching for clarity in the obscurity.

In the haze, every step felt tentative, each movement measured and deliberate. The path ahead was uncertain, much like the journey of starting anew when life insists on taking unexpected turns. It is in these moments of uncertainty that one must rely on an inner compass, a sense of direction that is not always visible but deeply felt.

The fog, with its soft embrace, forces an inward gaze. Stripped of the distractions of the visible world, the mind turns to introspection. Here lies the birthplace of reflection, where thoughts swirl like the mist, sometimes elusive, often profound. It is a space where questions arise, not always with answers, but with the potential for understanding.

What does it mean to begin again? It is more than a fresh start; it is a reimagining, a reconsideration of what is possible. It involves letting go of preconceived notions and embracing the unfamiliar. This process is not without its challenges. Fear of the unknown can be paralyzing, much like the fog that obscures the path. Yet, within this fear lies the opportunity for growth.

In the quiet of the mist, memories surface—some cherished, others painful. They are reminders of past experiences, lessons learned, and the resilience that has carried us through. These memories are the anchors that ground us, even as we navigate new beginnings. They offer perspective, a reminder that every ending is a prelude to a new chapter.

As I walked, the fog began to lift, revealing the landscape in soft, muted hues. It was as if the world was awakening, slowly unveiling its beauty. This gradual unveiling is much like the process of finding clarity within oneself. It requires patience and trust in the process, allowing time for the fog to dissipate and for vision to clear.

In these moments of clarity, there is a profound sense of connection—to oneself, to others, and to the world at large. It is a reminder that we are part of something greater, a tapestry of experiences woven together. Each thread is significant, contributing to the richness of the whole.

The journey through the fog is an invitation to pause, to breathe, and to reflect. It is a reminder that clarity often comes not in the rush, but in the stillness. It is in these quiet moments that we find the courage to move forward, to trust in our ability to navigate the unknown.

And so, as the fog lifts and the path becomes visible once more, there is a sense of readiness—a readiness to step forward, to re-begin at zero, and to embrace the infinite possibilities that lie ahead. The fog may return, as it often does, but with each encounter, there is the potential for renewed vision and deeper understanding.

The Lens of Truth

What if we could strip away the layers of illusion that cloud our perception, peeling back the veils that obscure reality? In this pursuit of clarity, the lens of truth becomes our most vital tool, allowing us to see the world not as it appears, but as it truly is.

The lens of truth is not a physical object one can grasp or hold. It exists within us, a perspective shift that requires courage and intention. This lens demands that we confront the narratives we've been told and the stories we tell ourselves. It challenges us to question the assumptions that have shaped our worldview, urging us to seek authenticity in a world often marred by facades.

Imagine gazing through this lens, seeing not just the surface but the intricate web of connections that bind us all. Each interaction, each choice, reverberates beyond the immediate moment, echoing through the lives of others in ways we may never fully comprehend. This interconnectedness is the essence of truth, a reminder that our actions, however small, are part of a larger tapestry.

Yet, adopting this lens is not without its challenges. It requires us to confront our own biases and prejudices, acknowledging the discomfort they bring. This process is akin to polishing a mirror, revealing imperfections we might prefer to ignore. But in embracing these imperfections, we begin to understand the complexity of our own humanity and that of others.

Through this lens, we begin to recognize the power of vulnerability. Truth is not an absolute; it is a mosaic of perspectives, each piece contributing to the whole. By sharing our own truths, we invite others to do the same, creating a space where honesty and empathy can flourish. This exchange is transformative, fostering connections that transcend superficial differences.

The lens of truth also invites us to reconsider our relationship with time. In a world that often glorifies speed and efficiency, this lens encourages us to slow down, to savour the present moment. It reminds us that truth is found not in the relentless pursuit of more, but in the quiet appreciation of what is. By grounding ourselves in the present, we open our eyes to the beauty that surrounds us, often hidden in plain sight.

As we navigate the complexities of life, the lens of truth serves as both guide and companion. It offers clarity amidst chaos and light in moments of darkness. It teaches us to listen deeply, to observe keenly, and to engage with the world with a sense of wonder and curiosity.

In this way, the lens of truth is not merely a tool, but a way of being. It invites us to live with integrity, to align our actions with our values, and to honour the inherent dignity of every individual we encounter. Through this lens, we find not only truth but also a deeper understanding of ourselves and our place in the world.

And so, with each step forward, we carry this lens with us, ever mindful of its power to transform our perceptions and, ultimately, our lives.

Focusing the Mind

The mind, much like the unbounded ocean, can be a tumultuous expanse. Thoughts drift like waves, sometimes crashing in chaotic patterns, other times gently lapping against the shores of our consciousness. In the vastness of this mental sea, finding focus can feel akin to navigating through a fog without a compass. Yet, it is within this very focus that we discover the tools to steer our lives with intention and clarity.

Imagine standing on the precipice of a new beginning, where the only certainty is the unfamiliar path ahead. Here, the mind's inclination is to wander into the recesses of uncertainty, where doubt and distraction dwell. To tether the mind in such moments, one must cultivate a sanctuary of stillness. By engaging in practices that anchor our awareness, we carve out a space where clarity can flourish amidst the noise.

In the quietude of early morning, when the world is still wrapped in slumber, there lies an opportunity to harness the mind's innate capacity for focus. It is in these moments, before the day's demands seep into our consciousness, that we can plant the seeds of intention. This is not about rigid discipline or forceful concentration, but rather about gentle guidance, like a shepherd tending to a flock.

The breath becomes an ally in this endeavour, a rhythmic companion that draws us back to the present. With each inhalation, we invite awareness, and with each exhalation, we release the clutter that clings to our thoughts. The mind, when anchored to the breath, starts to shed its layers of distraction, revealing the core of our being – a place where focus resides naturally.

Yet, focus is not a static state; it is a dynamic dance between attention and awareness. It acknowledges the presence of thoughts without succumbing to their pull. Like a skilled surfer riding the crest of a wave, we learn to navigate the ebb and flow of mental chatter. In this dance, we find our rhythm, a cadence that allows us to engage with life's complexities with grace.

To cultivate focus is to practice the art of letting go – of expectations, of judgments, of the need for perfection. The mind, when unburdened by these weights, finds its natural equilibrium. In this state, creativity blossoms, problem-solving becomes intuitive, and decisions are made with confidence.

As we nurture this focused state, we begin to notice the profound connection between mind and body. The two are not separate entities but are intricately intertwined, each influencing the other. When the mind is calm and focused, the body responds in kind, shedding tension and embracing ease.

In the tapestry of life, focus is the thread that weaves through our experiences, lending them coherence and meaning. It is not about shutting out the world but about being fully present within it, engaging with each moment as it unfolds. By focusing the mind, we step into a realm where possibilities abound, where the path forward is illuminated by the light of our attentive presence.

Thus, the practice of focusing the mind is not merely a skill to be mastered but a way of being in the world. It is an invitation to explore the depths of our consciousness, to find stillness amidst chaos, and to navigate life with a sense of purpose and clarity that guides us toward our true north.

Clarity in Purpose

As I sat on the worn wooden bench, the cool breeze gently tousling my hair, I pondered the significance of purpose. It's a word we often toss around casually, yet its depth is akin to the vast ocean, teeming with life yet mysterious in its depths. Purpose, I've realized, is not merely about what we set out to do; it's about understanding the very core of why we exist.

In the quiet moments, when the world fades to a soft hum, I find myself reflecting on the clarity of my own intentions. It is in these moments that I understand the importance of aligning my actions with my deepest values. This alignment, however, is not always straightforward. It requires peeling back layers of assumptions, expectations, and societal pressures that often cloud our vision.

I remember a pivotal moment when I stood at a crossroads, my mind a cacophony of possibilities and doubts. It was then that I learned the power of stillness. In the silence, I allowed my thoughts to settle, like silt in a glass of water. Slowly, the murky waters cleared, revealing a path that resonated with my inner truth. Clarity, I found, is not something to be attained through force but through gentle introspection.

Once I embraced this clarity, a profound shift occurred. Decisions that once felt burdensome became opportunities for growth. The weight of uncertainty lifted as I began to trust in my own compass. This trust, I realized, is essential. It is the faith that the choices I make, rooted in a clear purpose, will lead me to where I need to be.

Yet, clarity is not a destination—it is a continuous practice. It demands regular reflection and a willingness to recalibrate when necessary. Life, with its twists and turns, often challenges our sense of purpose. It is in these moments of doubt that I remind myself to return to my core, to the quiet space where my true intentions reside.

Our purpose is not a solitary endeavour. It intertwines with the lives of others, creating a tapestry of shared experiences and common goals. In recognizing this interconnectedness, I find a deeper sense of fulfilment. The clarity of my purpose is amplified when I contribute to something greater than myself.

Through this understanding, I have come to appreciate the beauty of small, deliberate actions. Each step, no matter how insignificant it may seem, is a thread in the larger fabric of my purpose. It is these threads that weave the story of my life, a story that is uniquely mine yet universally connected.

As the sun sets, casting a warm glow over the horizon, I am reminded of the cyclical nature of clarity. It ebbs and flows, much like the tides, but always returns, guiding me forward. In this ever-changing world, clarity in purpose is my anchor, grounding me in the present while gently nudging me toward the future.

In the end, I understand that clarity is not about having all the answers, but about asking the right questions. It is the courage to seek, to listen, and to trust in the unfolding of my path. And with each step, I find myself re-beginning at zero, embracing the infinite possibilities that clarity brings.

The Light of Understanding

In the quiet moments of reflection, there emerges a profound clarity that feels like the first rays of dawn breaking over a darkened landscape. This clarity does not arrive with fanfare or grand gestures; it seeps in gently, illuminating the shadows of confusion and doubt that have lingered for far too long. It is the light of understanding, a beacon that guides us through the often tumultuous waters of our own thoughts and emotions.

Understanding is not about having all the answers; rather, it is about seeing the questions more clearly. It is the recognition that life's complexities are not puzzles to be solved but experiences to be lived. With understanding comes a sense of peace, a realization that the chaos of the world is mirrored within us, and that by comprehending our inner landscapes, we can navigate the outer world with greater ease.

This light does not discriminate between the mundane and the profound. It shines equally on the small, everyday interactions as it does on the larger existential dilemmas. It reveals the interconnectedness of all things, showing us that each moment, each decision, each thought, and each feeling is part of a greater tapestry of existence. It is a reminder that we are not isolated islands but part of a vast ocean of shared experiences and emotions.

To cultivate this understanding, one must practice patience and openness. It requires a willingness to listen—not just to others, but to oneself. It involves peeling back the layers of preconceptions and biases that cloud our perceptions, allowing us to see things as they truly are, rather than as we wish them to be. It is an exercise in humility, acknowledging that our knowledge is incomplete and that there is always more to learn, more to see, more to feel.

As we embrace this light, we begin to see the world through a lens of compassion and empathy. We recognize the struggles of others as reflections of our own, understanding that beneath the surface differences, there is a shared humanity that binds us all. This awareness fosters a sense of connection and community, encouraging us to reach out to others with kindness and understanding.

In the process of understanding, we also learn to forgive—both ourselves and others. We realize that mistakes are not failures but opportunities for growth and learning. This forgiveness is not about condoning wrongdoing but about releasing the burden of anger and resentment that weighs us down, freeing us to move forward with a lighter heart.

Ultimately, the light of understanding is a transformative force. It changes the way we see ourselves and the world around us. It empowers us to live more authentically, to align our actions with our values, and to find meaning and purpose in even the most challenging circumstances. It is a gift that we give to ourselves, one that enriches our lives and the lives of those we touch.

In this journey of re-beginning at zero, understanding becomes the compass that guides us, the light that illuminates our path, and the gentle whisper that reminds us that we are never truly alone. It is the quiet yet powerful force that propels us forward, encouraging us to explore, to question, and to grow.

Chapter 14: The Path of Purpose

Discovering the Calling

In the quiet moments, when the world lulls itself into a gentle hum, we often find ourselves pondering the paths we walk. Life, with its myriad of choices and crossroads, is a vast tapestry woven with the threads of our decisions. It is in these moments of introspection that one might stumble upon the faint whisper of a calling.

For many, the idea of a calling is elusive, an enigmatic echo that reverberates through the corridors of the mind. It is not always a grand epiphany or a blazing revelation, but rather a subtle nudge—a tug at the soul urging exploration. This calling is not confined to the boundaries of profession or vocation; it transcends the tangible and ventures into the realm of purpose.

To discover this calling, one must first cultivate a sense of openness—a willingness to listen to the whispers of intuition that often go unheard amidst the cacophony of daily life. It requires a pause, a moment to step back and observe the patterns that emerge when the noise fades away.

In this pursuit, reflection becomes an invaluable ally. By examining the moments that ignite passion and joy, one can begin to discern the contours of their calling. These moments are not always grandiose; sometimes, they are the quiet satisfaction derived from a task well done or the deep fulfilment found in helping another.

The journey towards understanding one's calling is not always linear. It is a dance of trial and error, of venturing down paths that may lead to dead ends, yet each step taken is a step towards clarity. Within the missteps and detours lie lessons, each one illuminating the way forward.

At times, the calling may be shrouded in doubt, hidden beneath layers of fear and uncertainty. It requires courage to peel back these layers and confront the insecurities that may have kept it concealed. Yet, it is in this vulnerability that strength is forged, and the true essence of the calling is revealed.

For some, the calling is a quiet commitment to nurturing the world around them, be it through art, teaching, or the simple act of kindness. For others, it is a relentless pursuit of knowledge, a quest to unravel the mysteries of the universe. Whatever form it takes, the calling is a deeply personal journey, one that aligns with the values and truths held dear.

As one navigates this path, it becomes clear that the calling is not a destination but a continuous evolution. It adapts and grows, shaped by experiences and insights gained along the way. It is a lifelong companion, ever-present, guiding and challenging in equal measure.

In the end, discovering the calling is an invitation to live with intention, to craft a life that resonates with authenticity and purpose. It is an acknowledgment that within each of us lies a unique melody, waiting to be heard, nurtured, and shared with the world. And so, with each day, we listen a little more closely, attuning ourselves to the rhythm of our calling, ready to begin anew.

The Journey Towards Meaning

Reflecting on the essence of existence, one finds a tapestry woven with threads of questions, doubts, and aspirations. This intricate design, though complex, is what gives life its profound beauty. The quest for meaning, often considered a lifelong endeavour, is not about reaching a final destination but rather about finding purpose in the moments that fill our days.

It begins with the subtle whisperings of curiosity that nudge us to explore beyond the surface. These whispers encourage a deeper examination of our thoughts, actions, and the world around us. In this exploration, we discover the significance of small moments that often go unnoticed in the hustle of daily life. The laughter shared with a friend, the quiet satisfaction of a job well done, or the simple pleasure of a sunset—all contribute to the larger narrative of our existence.

Understanding meaning is akin to peeling away the layers of an onion. Each layer reveals new insights, and with each insight, there is a greater comprehension of oneself and one's place in the universe. It is through this process that one learns to appreciate the interconnectedness of all things. The realization that every action, no matter how minute, reverberates through the lives of others is both humbling and empowering.

In the pursuit of meaning, one often encounters challenges and obstacles. These are not merely hindrances but opportunities for growth and learning. The struggles we face can illuminate paths previously unseen, guiding us towards greater self-awareness and empathy. It is in overcoming adversity that we often find the most profound clarity and purpose.

As we navigate the complexities of life, it is essential to remain open to change. Flexibility and adaptability allow us to embrace new experiences and perspectives, enriching our understanding of the world. This openness fosters a sense of wonder and curiosity that keeps the spirit of exploration alive. Through this lens, even the mundane can become extraordinary, offering fresh insights and inspiration.

Moreover, connection with others plays a pivotal role in shaping our journey towards meaning. Relationships provide a mirror through which we can see ourselves more clearly. The bonds we form with family, friends, and even strangers, contribute to our understanding of love, compassion, and shared humanity. These connections remind us that we are not alone in our search for purpose.

In this reflective journey, it is crucial to cultivate a sense of gratitude. Recognizing and appreciating the abundance in our lives, regardless of how it manifests, can transform our perspective. Gratitude shifts focus from what we lack to what we possess, fostering a mindset that is both positive and resilient.

Ultimately, the pursuit of meaning is a deeply personal and evolving process. It requires patience, introspection, and the courage to confront the unknown. By embracing the journey with an open heart and mind, we create a rich tapestry of experiences that lead us closer to understanding our true selves. In this ongoing exploration, we find that the search for meaning is not a destination but a continuous unfolding of the self, enriched by every step taken along the way.

Aligning with Destiny

In the quiet moments of introspection, when the world fades and the mind turns inward, there lies a profound opportunity to connect with the essence of one's true path. This chapter invites a deep dive into the subtle art of aligning with destiny, a concept that transcends mere fate and becomes an active, deliberate pursuit of one's highest potential.

Destiny is often perceived as a predetermined path, an unalterable course set forth by forces beyond our control. However, upon closer examination, it reveals itself as a dynamic interplay between choice and circumstance, a delicate dance that requires both awareness and intention. The journey to align with destiny thus begins with an awakening to the present moment, an acknowledgment of the intricate web of experiences, relationships, and decisions that have brought us to our current state.

Reflection becomes the cornerstone of this alignment. It is through the lens of introspection that we can discern the patterns and themes that consistently emerge in our lives. These patterns, often overlooked, are the whispers of destiny, guiding us toward our true calling. By cultivating a practice of mindful reflection, we gain insight into our authentic desires and aspirations, the seeds of our destiny waiting to be nurtured.

As we navigate the labyrinth of life, obstacles and challenges serve as signposts, not deterrents. Each setback, each moment of uncertainty, is an invitation to reassess and realign. It is in these moments that resilience is forged, and clarity emerges. By embracing these challenges with an open heart and a curious mind, we tap into an inner wisdom that steers us back onto our destined path.

Moreover, aligning with destiny requires a harmonious relationship with time. It involves shedding the weight of past regrets and the anxiety of future uncertainties, anchoring oneself firmly in the now. This present-centeredness allows for a receptivity to the subtle nudges of intuition, those fleeting moments of insight that illuminate the way forward. Trusting in this inner guidance, we learn to make choices that resonate with our core values and deepest truths.

Community, too, plays a pivotal role in this alignment. Surrounding oneself with individuals who inspire, challenge, and support us creates a fertile environment for growth and self-discovery. Within these connections, we find mirrors that reflect our strengths and areas for growth, offering perspectives that enrich our understanding of our place in the world.

Ultimately, aligning with destiny is an ongoing process, a continual recalibration as we evolve and grow. It is marked by a balance between surrender and action, an acceptance of what is, and a proactive engagement with what could be. In this space between acceptance and ambition, we find the freedom to redefine success, not in terms of external achievements, but as a deep-seated sense of fulfilment and purpose.

In the grand tapestry of existence, each thread of experience weaves into the fabric of destiny, creating a unique pattern that is ours alone. By aligning with this pattern, we step into a life that is not only meaningful but also deeply resonant with the essence of who we are. This alignment does not promise a life without challenges, but it offers the assurance of a journey that is profoundly authentic and uniquely our own.

The Compass of Values

In the quiet moments of reflection, when the world demands less of our attention, a subtle whisper often beckons us to consider the essence of who we truly are. This whisper is no mere figment of imagination but an invitation to explore the guiding principles that shape our actions and decisions. In the vast landscape of our internal world, values stand as the compass, providing direction amid the chaos of life's myriad choices.

Values are not static; they evolve with experiences, insights, and the passage of time. They are the invisible threads that weave through the fabric of our lives, influencing our perceptions and interactions. To understand one's values is to hold a mirror up to the soul, reflecting the deepest desires and convictions that reside within.

This exploration requires courage, for it may reveal contradictions and conflicts between our professed values and our actions. It is in these moments of dissonance that growth is nurtured. Embracing this discomfort allows us to realign our path, ensuring that our actions resonate with our core beliefs.

As we navigate the complexities of modern existence, it becomes increasingly imperative to articulate and understand our values. The ever-present noise of societal expectations and external pressures can easily obscure our internal compass. Yet, when we take the time to articulate what truly matters, we find clarity and purpose.

In the dance of life, where change is the only constant, values offer a sense of stability. They are the anchor that grounds us, allowing us to weather the storms of uncertainty with grace and resilience. As we delve into this introspective journey, we discover that values are not just individual markers but communal ones, connecting us to a larger tapestry of shared human experience.

Consider the moments of profound connection with others—those instances where words are unnecessary, and a shared understanding prevails. These are the moments when our values align with those of others, creating a harmonious symphony of human connection. Recognizing this interconnectedness fosters empathy and compassion, bridging the divide between self and other.

As we align our actions with our values, we cultivate authenticity. This authenticity becomes a beacon, attracting those who resonate with similar principles and guiding us toward endeavours that fulfil our deepest aspirations. When we live in accordance with our values, we experience a sense of integrity and congruence, where our outer world mirrors our inner convictions.

Yet, the path of values is not without its challenges. It requires vigilance and a willingness to question the status quo. It demands that we remain open to the possibility of change, to the idea that our values may shift as we grow and evolve. This flexibility is not a sign of weakness but of strength, reflecting a deep commitment to living a life true to oneself.

In the end, the exploration of values is a deeply personal endeavour, one that invites us to engage with the world from a place of authenticity and purpose. It is a journey that, while deeply individual, resonates with the universal quest for meaning and fulfilment. As we chart this course, we come to realize that our values are not just a reflection of who we are but a powerful force that shapes the world we inhabit.

Living with Intention

In a world that often seems to whirl us around in a chaotic dance, it is easy to find ourselves swept away by the currents of circumstance. We may wake up one day and realize that the life we are living is not the one we envisioned. It is in these moments of clarity that we understand the necessity of living with intention.

Living with intention is not about meticulous planning or rigid control. It is about becoming aware of the choices we make and aligning them with our deeper values and desires. It is the art of pausing amidst the noise to listen to the quiet whispers of our heart, guiding us towards a more meaningful existence.

To live intentionally, we must first cultivate awareness. This involves taking the time to reflect on our daily actions and the motivations behind them. Are we doing things out of habit, obligation, or fear? Or are our actions driven by passion, curiosity, and a sense of purpose? By examining these motivations, we can begin to disentangle ourselves from patterns that do not serve us.

It is also essential to set clear intentions. These are not to-do lists or goals, but rather guiding principles that shape our actions and decisions. Intentions are rooted in the present moment and reflect our core values. They act as a compass, steering us towards a life that resonates with our true self.

Consider the power of beginning each day with a simple intention. It could be as straightforward as "Today, I will approach my work with creativity," or "I will listen deeply to those around me." These intentions serve as gentle reminders to stay aligned with our values, even when the world around us seems determined to pull us in different directions.

Living intentionally also means embracing mindfulness. This practice allows us to fully engage with our experiences, whether they are mundane or extraordinary. By being present, we open ourselves up to the richness of life, savouring moments that might otherwise pass unnoticed. Mindfulness enables us to appreciate the beauty in simplicity and find gratitude in the ordinary.

However, living with intention is not without its challenges. It requires courage and vulnerability to confront our fears and resist the societal pressures that often dictate the "right" path. It involves continual self-reflection and the willingness to make changes, even when it is uncomfortable.

Yet, the rewards of intentional living are profound. It brings a sense of fulfilment and peace, as we no longer feel like passive participants in our own lives. Instead, we become active creators, shaping a reality that is uniquely ours. Our relationships deepen, as we connect with others from a place of authenticity and presence.

Ultimately, living with intention is an ongoing practice. It is a commitment to ourselves and our dreams, a promise to live each day with purpose and meaning. As we navigate the complexities of life, let us carry this intention within us, guiding us towards a future that reflects the deepest truths of who we are. In doing so, we find a sense of liberation, as we step boldly into a life that is not only lived but truly cherished.

Chapter 15: The Celebration of Renewal

Embracing the New

There is an undeniable allure to the blank canvas, a space of infinite possibilities where creativity and potential flourish. In the realm of new beginnings, we find ourselves often caught between the comfort of the known and the thrill of the undiscovered. It is in these moments that we must pause, reflect, and allow ourselves to be vulnerable to the unfamiliar.

Change is the catalyst that propels us forward, yet it can also be a source of trepidation. There is a natural tendency to cling to the past, to the familiar patterns and routines that have shaped our lives. However, growth demands that we release our grasp on what was and open our arms to what could be. This shift in mindset is not an easy task; it requires courage, resilience, and a willingness to step outside our comfort zones.

As we stand at the threshold of the new, it's essential to cultivate a mindset of curiosity and openness. Curiosity fuels innovation; it invites us to explore uncharted territories and discover hidden strengths within ourselves. When we approach life with a sense of wonder, each experience becomes an opportunity for learning and transformation.

Reflecting on past experiences, we often find that the most significant moments of growth occurred when we dared to take risks, to make decisions that defied conventional wisdom. These instances of boldness are not without fear or uncertainty, but they are driven by the belief that something greater awaits us on the other side. It is this belief that empowers us to move forward, even when the path ahead is shrouded in ambiguity.

The journey toward the new is not a solitary endeavour. Along the way, we encounter individuals who inspire, challenge, and support us. These connections are vital; they provide us with different perspectives and remind us that we are not alone in our quest for reinvention. By engaging with others, we expand our horizons and gain insights that enrich our understanding.

In this pursuit of the new, we must also recognize the importance of patience and self-compassion. Change does not occur overnight, and the process of transformation can be fraught with setbacks and detours. Embracing the new requires us to be gentle with ourselves, to acknowledge our progress, no matter how incremental it may seem. It is through this grace that we find the strength to persevere and the motivation to continue our journey.

Ultimately, the act of embracing the new is a testament to our resilience and adaptability. It is an affirmation of our capacity to evolve, to redefine our lives in ways that align with our deepest values and aspirations. As we navigate the complexities of change, let us remember that each beginning holds the promise of renewal, a chance to reimagine our futures and create lives that reflect our truest selves.

In this space of new beginnings, we are called to be architects of our destinies, to craft narratives that honor our past while celebrating the potential of what lies ahead. It is here, at the intersection of the old and the new, that we find the courage to re-begin at zero, to start anew with hope and determination as our guiding stars.

The Joy of Rebirth

There is a profound beauty in the art of beginning anew, a beauty that often lies hidden beneath layers of fear and uncertainty. It is a beauty that emerges quietly, like the first light of dawn breaking through the darkness, gently illuminating a path previously unseen. As we stand at the threshold of this new existence, we are gifted the rare opportunity to redefine who we are, to cast aside the burdens of our past selves, and to step forward into the unknown with a heart filled with hope.

In this delicate process, we find ourselves shedding the skin of our former lives, much like a snake discards its old skin to reveal a more vibrant and resilient form. This transformation is not without its challenges, yet it is within these very trials that we discover the strength and resilience we never knew we possessed. Each obstacle surmounted, each fear faced, becomes a stepping stone towards a more authentic existence.

At the core of rebirth lies the element of choice. We are given the chance to choose, to decide which aspects of our past we wish to carry forward and which we are ready to release. This choice is both liberating and daunting, for it requires us to confront the parts of ourselves we have long ignored or denied. Yet, in doing so, we pave the way for a future that is not merely an extension of our past but a canvas upon which we can paint our dreams anew.

The essence of rebirth is not in the grand gestures or sweeping changes but in the subtle shifts of perspective that alter our understanding of the world and our place within it. It is in the quiet moments of reflection, in the gentle whispers of our inner voice guiding us towards a path that resonates with our true nature. It is in the realization that we are not bound by the limitations of our past but are free to create a life that aligns with our deepest values and desires.

In this state of renewal, we become acutely aware of the interconnectedness of all things. Our rebirth is not an isolated event but a part of the greater cycle of life, a cycle that mirrors the natural world around us. Just as the seasons change, bringing with them new life and growth, so too do we evolve, shedding our old selves to make way for the new.

There is a quiet joy in this process, a joy that comes from the recognition that we are, in essence, returning to our true selves. It is a joy that transcends the fleeting pleasures of the material world, a joy that is rooted in the profound understanding that we are part of something much larger than ourselves.

As we navigate this path of rebirth, we do so with a sense of gratitude for the experiences that have shaped us, for the lessons we have learned, and for the opportunity to begin again. With each step forward, we embrace the unknown with open hearts, trusting that the journey will lead us to a place of deeper connection and fulfilment. This is the joy of rebirth, a joy that is both a destination and a journey, a journey that begins anew with each breath, with each moment, with each choice we make.

A Fresh Start

In the quiet moments of dawn, when the world is still wrapped in the soft embrace of sleep, there lies a unique opportunity to reset, to begin anew. It is in these moments that the mind finds clarity, unburdened by the noise of the day, and open to the possibilities that lie ahead.

As we stand at the precipice of change, there is a subtle whisper that beckons us to let go of what was and reach for what could be. The past, with its tangled web of experiences and emotions, has shaped us, but it does not define the path forward. Instead, it serves as a tapestry of lessons, gently reminding us of our resilience and capacity for growth.

The concept of starting over can be daunting, a vast expanse of unknowns stretching out before us. Yet, within this expanse lies the essence of potential. Each step taken towards a new beginning is a testament to the courage that resides within, a silent acknowledgment that we are capable of more than we often give ourselves credit for.

Consider the first brushstroke on a blank canvas. It is tentative, perhaps even hesitant, but it is a commitment to creation. The same can be said for the initial steps in crafting a new chapter in life. It is not about erasing what came before but rather about building upon it, infusing it with the vibrancy of newfound insight and perspective.

There is a quiet power in recognizing that each day offers a chance to recalibrate, to realign with our true selves. By shedding the weight of expectations—both external and internal—we gift ourselves the freedom to explore paths that resonate most deeply with our authentic desires.

In moments of reflection, we may find ourselves questioning the choices that led us to this point, wondering if the path we've taken aligns with the person we wish to become. This introspection is not an indulgence but a necessary step in forging ahead with intention. It is through this process of self-examination that we uncover the truths that will guide us in crafting a life that feels genuinely ours.

As we venture into this fresh start, let us not be afraid to dream boldly. The boundaries that once seemed insurmountable can dissolve when approached with a mindset of possibility. We are architects of our destinies, equipped with the tools of hope, determination, and an unwavering belief in our ability to thrive.

Let us cherish the uncertainty that accompanies new beginnings, for it is within this uncertainty that we find the seeds of innovation and transformation. Embracing the unknown with open arms allows us to tap into reservoirs of creativity and resilience that we may not have realized existed.

In this space of renewal, let us cultivate patience and compassion, both towards ourselves and others. Progress is not always linear, and setbacks are merely stepping stones on the path to a more fulfilling existence. With each new dawn, we are given the chance to redefine what success means to us, to reshape our narratives, and to step confidently into the future that awaits.

As we chart this course, may we find solace in the knowledge that the journey is uniquely ours, a testament to our spirit and the endless possibilities that lie ahead. The canvas is ours to paint, and the story is ours to write.

The Dance of Renewal

In the tapestry of life, renewal is a thread that weaves through every experience, every emotion, and every moment of transformation. It is a dance, intricate and graceful, that invites us to step onto the floor of change with open hearts and willing spirits. At the core of this dance lies the understanding that renewal is not a destination but a continuous process—one that requires presence, patience, and a willingness to surrender to the flow.

As the seasons turn, so do the cycles of our lives, inviting us to shed what no longer serves us and to welcome the new with curiosity and courage. This cycle of letting go and embracing anew is akin to the shedding of leaves by trees in autumn, creating space for fresh growth in spring. It is a natural rhythm, a reminder that life is ever-evolving, and that our capacity for renewal is boundless.

To engage in this dance is to cultivate a deep sense of awareness. It calls upon us to listen to the whispers of our inner selves, to recognize the subtle shifts in our desires, values, and dreams. It is in these quiet moments of introspection that we often find the seeds of renewal—small yet potent, waiting to be nurtured into fruition. By honouring these seeds, we acknowledge the potential for transformation that resides within us.

In the dance of renewal, vulnerability becomes a trusted partner. It is through vulnerability that we discover the courage to release the familiar and step into the unknown. This release is not always easy, for it requires us to confront fears and uncertainties that may have long been buried.

Yet, it is in embracing this vulnerability that we find strength and resilience, allowing us to move forward with grace and authenticity.

Every step in this dance is an opportunity for growth and learning. Each misstep or stumble is a lesson, guiding us toward greater understanding and self-awareness. It is a reminder that perfection is not the goal; rather, it is the journey of renewal itself that enriches our lives and deepens our connection to the world around us.

As we navigate this dance, we are reminded of the interconnectedness of all things. The renewal we experience within ourselves ripples outward, influencing the relationships and communities we are a part of. It is a testament to the power of renewal to inspire and uplift, to create spaces for healing and hope.

This dance is not solitary; it is a shared experience, a collective rhythm that binds us together in our humanity. As we engage in the dance of renewal, we are part of a larger narrative, one that celebrates the beauty of transformation and the endless possibilities that arise from it.

In the end, renewal is a dance that invites us to live fully and authentically, to embrace change with open arms and open hearts. It is a dance that celebrates the infinite potential within each of us, a reminder that we are always capable of beginning anew. As the music plays and the dance continues, we find ourselves not only participants but creators, shaping our lives with every step we take.

The Cycle Continues

In the ebb and flow of existence, the notion of cycles is omnipresent, weaving through the fabric of our lives with an unwavering rhythm. As the earth spins on its axis and the seasons transition from one to the next, so too do our lives circle back upon themselves, each conclusion a prelude to another beginning. This cyclical nature is both a comfort and a challenge, a testament to the enduring resilience and adaptability inherent in the human spirit.

Within these cycles lies a profound lesson: the understanding that every end is not a termination, but rather a transformation. It invites us to view our experiences, not as isolated incidents, but as interconnected segments of a grander narrative. This perspective can be both liberating and daunting, for it compels us to confront the continuity of our actions and the repercussions they bring forth.

In the throes of change, there is a temptation to cling to the familiar, to resist the pull of the unknown. Yet, it is within the unknown that growth resides. To step into the next cycle is to embrace the potential for renewal, to welcome the opportunity to redefine oneself within the context of new beginnings. The cycle is not merely a repetition of the past but a chance to reimagine the future.

This concept challenges us to cultivate awareness and intentionality, to recognize the patterns that emerge within our lives and to discern which patterns serve us and which hinder our progress. It is a call to conscious living, to the deliberate crafting of our narratives with the wisdom gleaned from previous cycles. In this way, we become architects of our destinies, actively shaping the course of our lives with each choice we make.

As we navigate these cycles, it is essential to honour the lessons learned and to carry them forward, allowing them to inform and guide our journey. Each cycle leaves its mark, an indelible imprint that shapes our perspectives and influences our actions. By acknowledging and integrating these lessons, we build a foundation of resilience and wisdom that fortifies us against the uncertainties that lie ahead.

The cycle's essence lies not in its predictability but in its potential for metamorphosis. It is an invitation to shed the skins of the past, to release the burdens that weigh us down and to step boldly into the light of possibility. This cyclical dance is a testament to the enduring power of hope, a reminder that, regardless of the challenges we face, there is always the potential for rebirth, for starting anew.

In embracing the cycle, we find solace in the knowledge that we are part of a larger tapestry, one that transcends the individual and connects us to the collective human experience. It is this interconnectedness that imbues our lives with meaning and purpose, reminding us that we are never truly alone in our struggles or triumphs. As the cycle continues, we are called to engage with life fully, to embrace its complexities and to find beauty in the ever-unfolding journey of becoming.

EPILOGUE

As the sun dips below the horizon, casting a warm glow over the landscape of our lives, we pause to reflect on the path we've traversed in the pages of this book. "Re-Begin at Zero" has invited us to peel back the layers of assumptions and inherited narratives that have long shaped our perceptions. Each chapter has been a gentle nudge towards the possibility of living today with a fresh perspective, unburdened by the weight of yesterday's shadows. In our exploration, we've learned to recognize the subtle yet pervasive influences of beliefs and biases that have coloured our world. The realization that these are not immutable truths but rather constructs of our own making is both liberating and empowering. It is this newfound awareness that grants us the courage to dismantle these constructs, to clear the slate, and to draft our own narrative, one that is authentic and true to our essence. Throughout our journey, we've encountered the stories of others who have taken this bold step towards renewal. Their experiences serve as both inspiration and testament to the transformative power of releasing the past. We've seen how shedding the weight of accumulated baggage allows for a lighter, more present existence, where each moment is met with openness and curiosity. The invitation to live only today is not a call to forget the past but rather to reframe it, to learn from it without letting it dictate our future. It is an invitation to engage with the world in a way that is mindful and intentional, to appreciate the beauty of the present moment without the interference of preconceived notions. As we close this book, the final pages serve not as an end but as a beginning, a starting point from which we can continue to explore the depths of our own potential. With each day, we have the opportunity to re-begin at zero, to approach life with a sense of wonder and possibility, unencumbered by the constraints of the past. This is the essence of living only today, and it is within reach for each of us who dares to take that first step.

www.ingramcontent.com/pod-product-compliance
Lightning Source LLC
Chambersburg PA
CBHW062139160726
48282CB00027B/874
* 9 7 8 9 3 3 4 3 8 5 6 1 8 *